CHAMBER PIECE

T0321805

Caroline Bird

CHAMBER PIECE

A pitch-black comedy

OBERON BOOKS
LONDON

WWW.OBERONBOOKS.COM

First published in 2013 by Oberon Books Ltd
521 Caledonian Road, London N7 9RH
Tel: +44 (0) 20 7607 3637 / Fax: +44 (0) 20 7607 3629
e-mail: info@oberonbooks.com
www.oberonbooks.com

A catalogue record for this book is available from the British Library.

PB ISBN: 978-1-78319-070-6
E ISBN: 978-1-78319-569-5

Cover design by Clement Graphics

Converted
by CPI Group (UK) Ltd, Croydon, CR0 4YY.

CHARACTERS

GOVERNOR
Female. Early thirties.

PHYSICIAN
Male. Early thirties.

RICHARD SANGER
Condemned inmate. Late twenties.

JOHN SANGER
Inmate's brother. Twenties.

AMY WATKINS
Identical twin sister of the murder victim, Tara
Watkins. Late teens.

WARDEN SUNSHINE
Female. New to the job.

WARDEN HEATHER
Female. Ex-prisoner.

WARDEN ALEX
Male. Ex-Community Support Officer.

JOURNALIST
Female.

SPIRITUAL ADVISOR
Male.

Chamber Piece by Caroline Bird was originally produced by the Lyric Hammersmith and first performed on 22 October 2013 as Show 3 of Secret Theatre.

The cast was as follows:

WARDEN SUNSHINE: Nadia Albina
WARDEN ALEX: Hammed Animashaun
RICHARD SANGER: Leo Bill
GOVERNOR: Cara Horgan
WARDEN HEATHER: Charlotte Josephine
JOURNALIST: Adelle Leonce
AMY WATKINS: Katherine Pearce
JOHN SANGER: Billy Seymour
SPIRITUAL ADVISOR: Sergo Vares
PHYSICIAN: Steven Webb

Director: Sean Holmes
Designer: Paul Wills
Lighting Designer: Lizzie Powell
Sound Designer: Nick Manning
Assistant Director: Ilinca Radulia

Secret Theatre Company: Nadia Albina, Hammed Animashaun, Leo Bill, Caroline Bird, Sean Holmes, Cara Horgan, Joel Horwood, Charlotte Josephine, Arinze Kene, Adelle Leonce, Nick Manning, Ellen McDougall, Katherine Pearce, Lizzie Powell, Billy Seymour, Hyemi Shin, Hayley Squires, Simon Stephens, Sergo Vares and Steven Webb.

SETTING FOR ACT ONE

The stage is divided into two rooms: the Execution Room (stage left) and the Witness Area (stage right). There is a small window on the adjoining wall – to allow the witnesses to watch the execution. On the far side of each room is a corridor area, so the characters can stand in the doorways, or huddle outside.

THE EXECUTION ROOM:

A white leather gurney with straps.

A heart monitor (screen facing away from the audience).

Two wheeled 'stands' clearly labelled 'A' and 'B' (each designed to hold eight syringes in separate slots). Stand A and B both contain 8 syringes clearly labelled from 1-8.

A drip chamber.

At the back is a door marked 'Chemical Room.'

THE WITNESS AREA:

Two rows of red plastic chairs facing the window.

Boxes of tissues strategically placed.

Note:

The gurney in the execution room should be tilted upwards towards the audience – so the inmate is strapped into a crucifixion-type pose. Even when the execution chamber is blacked out, the gurney should still be lit by a dim spotlight.

This play is set in a version of modern Britain,
sometime in the near future.

ACT ONE

WITNESS ROOM

JOURNALIST and GOVERNOR are in the middle of an informal interview. JOURNALIST has her notepad open on her lap. SPIRITUAL ADVISOR is observing quietly.

JOURNALIST: Are you pioneering a legal voyage towards a safer Britain?

GOVERNOR: That's a question for the politicians – but last year was an experiment and now we're a hop and a jump away from a permanent wing with a chapel and two lounge areas.

JOURNALIST: Once funding is finalised.

GOVERNOR: Which it will be.

JOURNALIST: Next stop, world domination?

GOVERNOR: *(At speed.)* Oh Grace, I can't leap straight from Governing Governor of here to CEO of the National Offenders Management Service!

JOURNALIST: I was being flip…

GOVERNOR: *(Interrupting.)* Perhaps in a map-cap dream I could move into Area Management next year, become Director of Operation within two years, Deputy Director General in four, then land the top job – still pert – at the age of thirty-six. *(Little laugh.)* I don't know, I haven't thought about it much to be honest.

JOURNALIST: You sound like you've given it *some* thought.

Enter AMY.

GOVERNOR: *(To JOURNALIST.)* I'm so glad you're here to witness our process. I say to my staff: 'be prepared, calm and quick. In this work, efficiency is kindness.'

A dim light illuminates the gurney in the adjoining Execution Room. Audience suddenly realises where they are.

GOVERNOR waits for JOURNALIST to write in her notebook.

AMY: Where should I sit?

GOVERNOR: *(Dictating.)* Efficiency is kindness.

JOURNALIST reluctantly writes it down.

(To AMY.) Who are you here for, sweetness?

AMY: I'm Tara's sister.

GOVERNOR: Front row. *(To AMY and JOURNALIST.)* Mobiles please.

AMY hands over her phone.

JOURNALIST hands over her phone.

GOVERNOR puts her hand out again.

JOURNALIST coolly hands over another phone and a mini tablet.

SPIRITUAL ADVISOR makes a gesture meaning 'I'm exempt.'

SPIRITUAL ADVISOR: Spiritual advisor.

GOVERNOR blinks at him.

Enter JOHN, all dressed in black.

AMY turns to look at him.

GOVERNOR: *(To JOHN.)* Phone.

JOHN hands over his phone.

(To JOHN, quietly, pointing at the back row of chairs.) If I were you, I'd sit at the back.

(Loudly, to EVERYONE, waving the phones.) I'll return them at the end.

Exit GOVERNOR.

Blackout on the Witness Room.

EXECUTION ROOM

The WARDENS unlock the cell door, haul RICHARD out, and march him to the Execution Room. He drags his feet.

All three WARDENS strap him to the gurney.

WARDEN SUNSHINE attaches the heart monitor leads to RICHARD's chest.

WARDEN HEATHER inserts one IV line into RICHARD's arm.

While all this is happening, this scene is simultaneously occurring in the Witness Room:

WITNESS ROOM

JOHN walks up to the glass and stares intently at his brother on the gurney.

JOHN: *(Whispering.)* Rich, Richie, Richard.

RICHARD doesn't look at him.

Enter PHYSICIAN. He walks in swiftly with his head down, positions himself at the front then turns to face the witnesses.

PHYSICIAN: My name is Dr Swan and I can answer any queries you may have. I know this is a potentially stressful time, and I want you to feel you can talk to me.

JOHN: Shouldn't you be in there?

PHYSICIAN: Unfortunately no working physician can ethically assist with such an event.

JOHN: *(To PHYSICIAN.)* But his straps look too tight.

PHYSICIAN: I'm sure they're elasticated.

JOHN: Check.

PHYSICIAN: Checking would count as 'assisting.' It's tricky to explain.

AMY: He hopes the straps *are* too tight.

PHYSICIAN: That's not what I said.

AMY: He's being tactful.

PHYSICIAN: I care for all people.

JOHN: Off you go then.

PHYSICIAN: Much as I sympathise…

AMY: *Sympathise?*

PHYSICIAN: Let's start again.

JOHN: What if he dies in pain?

AMY: Dies in pain? Who the fuck are you?

JOHN: He's my brother.

AMY: *(To PHYSICIAN.)* I don't want him here.

PHYSICIAN: It's only seven minutes, let's not over-react.

AMY: OVERREACT?!!

PHYSICIAN: *(Pointing at the SPIRITUAL ADVISOR.)* We also have an in-house counsellor, thank you.

SPIRITUAL ADVISOR: Spiritual Advisor.

PHYSICIAN: He can answer queries too.

PHYSICIAN sits down immediately.

AMY: Is that it?

PHYSICIAN does not look open to any more questions.

JOHN: *(To the window.)* Rich. Richie. Are you alright, Richie?

JOHN waves his hands at the window.

AMY looks at PHYSICIAN as if to say 'do something.'

PHYSICIAN: Don't wave.

JOHN stops waving.

JOURNALIST writes something down.

Enter GOVERNOR. She takes a seat at the back – like a theatre director watching her own press night.

EXECUTION ROOM

Preparations are now complete.

WARDEN ALEX picks up the phone.

WARDEN ALEX: This is Warden Alex Cooper calling from the chamber.

He listens for a moment.

WARDEN ALEX puts down the phone.

Switch on the PA.

WARDEN HEATHER switches on the PA system.

WITNESS ROOM

JOHN: Oh god.

GOVERNOR gives the WARDENS the thumbs up.

During the execution, GOVERNOR subconsciously mouths the official words and plays out the actions with her hands.

EXECUTION ROOM

WARDEN ALEX: *(To the witnesses.)* The time is *(Looks at the clock and waits for two seconds.)* 17.30, October 21st, exactly in accordance with the specified time on the death warrant issued by the court. There have been no stays or reprieves. Richard Sanger, do you have any last words, to be broadcast to the witness gallery?

Long pause.

RICHARD: No.

(In the Witness Room, the JOURNALIST drops her pen down onto her notebook and mutters 'fuck's sake.' JOHN starts to cry.)

WARDEN ALEX: Please switch off the PA.

WARDEN HEATHER switches off the PA system.

The execution has begun.

WARDEN SUNSHINE is the designated executioner.

She removes syringe 1 from the stand and pushes the entire contents into the medication port of the cannula.

WARDEN SUNSHINE: One.

When the syringe is empty, she hands it to WARDEN HEATHER for safe disposal.

RICHARD closes his eyes.

WARDEN HEATHER: And the eyes have closed.

WARDEN SUNSHINE now removes syringe 2 from the stand and repeats the process.

WARDEN SUNSHINE: Two.

WARDEN SUNSHINE hands over the empty syringe.

WARDEN SUNSHINE picks up syringe 3, administers, hands it over.

Three.

WARDEN HEATHER: *(Whispering.)* Count in your head.

WARDEN HEATHER now examines RICHARD's face.

No signs of consciousness.

Convinced, she nods to WARDEN SUNSHINE to continue.

WARDEN ALEX is observing the heart monitor screen.

WARDEN SUNSHINE repeats this process with the rest of the syringes; all the while, she is mouthing the count: Three, Four etc.

This takes as long as it takes.

Syringe 7 and 8 contain potassium chloride, the lethal injection.

After 7, WARDEN ALEX looks up calmly from the heart monitor.

He gestures to WARDEN HEATHER to check the electrodes are connected to the inmate.

WARDEN HEATHER confirms they are.

Finally, WARDEN SUNSHINE administers the eighth syringe.

Her face shows palpable relief.

WARDEN ALEX: Please close the drapes.

WARDEN HEATHER closes the drapes.

Lights down on the Witness Room.

ALL WARDENS heave big sighs of relief.

WARDEN ALEX: Well done guys.

WARDEN SUNSHINE: I need a cigarette.

WARDEN HEATHER: That's the worst part over.

WARDEN ALEX: It's like unloading boxes from here on.

WARDEN HEATHER: You did well.

WARDEN ALEX: *(To WARDEN SUNSHINE.)* Now send us home.

WARDEN SUNSHINE: What was your last line?

WARDEN ALEX: 'Please close the drapes.'

WARDEN SUNSHINE: *(In an official voice.)* And call the physician.

WARDEN ALEX looks at the heart monitor screen.

WARDEN ALEX: That's not right.

WARDEN SUNSHINE: *(Suddenly panicked.)* Sorry. *(Official voice.)* Time of death: 17.38.

WARDEN ALEX: Wrong.

WARDEN SUNSHINE: 37?

WARDEN ALEX: Stop.

WARDEN SUNSHINE: What have I forgotten?

WARDEN ALEX: *(Pointing at the heart monitor.)* Look.

WARDEN SUNSHINE and WARDEN HEATHER look at the heart monitor screen.

Slight pause.

They look at it again.

WARDEN SUNSHINE: Is it broken?

WARDEN HEATHER: Maybe it's jammed.

WARDEN ALEX: It's not a printer.

WARDEN SUNSHINE: Maybe it's processing.

WARDEN HEATHER: Processing what?

WARDEN SUNSHINE: The situation.

WARDEN HEATHER: Processing the situation?

WARDEN SUNSHINE: I don't know do I?

WARDEN ALEX hits the heart monitor (as if it's a dodgy washing machine.)

They look again.

WARDEN ALEX: Check his wrist.

WARDEN HEATHER tries to find the inmate's pulse.

WARDEN HEATHER: Which vein do I press?

WARDEN SUNSHINE: Not with your thumb…

WARDEN HEATHER: You do it then, genius.

WARDEN SUNSHINE checks his pulse.

WARDEN SUNSHINE: Shit.

WARDEN HEATHER: Is it faint though? Like a tiny flicker?

WARDEN SUNSHINE: What do you mean?

WARDEN HEATHER: Like an after-death kind of thing?

WARDEN ALEX: An after-death pulse?

WARDEN HEATHER: No like when they used to cut people's heads off, but their mouths would carry on talking for a bit.

WARDEN SUNSHINE: That never, ever happened.

WARDEN HEATHER: Yes it did.

WARDEN SUNSHINE: It just feels normal.

WARDEN HEATHER: Nice work new girl.

WARDEN SUNSHINE: *(To WARDEN HEATHER.)* You prepared the potions.

WARDEN HEATHER: I'm experienced. I'm an old hand.

WARDEN ALEX: Heather, you've done it *once* before.

WARDEN HEATHER: Once before? Oh like Christopher Columbus only discovered America 'once before'? Like Einstein only figured out… the thing 'once before'? And don't call them potions like we're twelve, mixing toothpaste with lavender water. I know my chemicals: Sodium Penthonal (5 grams between 2 syringes, 2.5 grams each,) 40ml saline solution, 50mgs muscle relaxer, then the Potassium Chloride: 240.

WARDEN ALEX: 240 what?

WARDEN HEATHER: *(Straining a little.)* mEq.

WARDEN ALEX: Stands for?

Slight pause.

WARDEN HEATHER: I've got a photographic memory, I'm seeing 'mEq'.

WARDEN ALEX checks the clipboard.

Anyway, if we gave him too much he'd definitely be de…

WARDEN ALEX: *(Interrupting.)* Milliequivalents.

WARDEN HEATHER: That's exactly what I put in, mate.

WARDEN ALEX: So what happened? You can't survive a drug that stops your heart.

GOVERNOR knocks on the door.

WARDEN HEATHER: *(Urgent whisper.)* Don't you dare tell her.

WARDEN ALEX opens it a crack.

WARDEN ALEX: Ma'am?

GOVERNOR: The curtain closed, but no call. Do you want him?

WARDEN ALEX: Who?

GOVERNOR: The physician? To pronounce it?

WARDEN ALEX: We just have to…clean the… *(Has no idea what to say.)*

GOVERNOR: Defecation?

WARDEN ALEX: Hey?

GOVERNOR: Defecation was it?

WARDEN ALEX: *(Bewildered.)* Right.

GOVERNOR: The anguish of death.

WARDEN ALEX: What?

GOVERNOR: I said that would be the anguish of death. Makes you let go. Use as many antiseptic wipes as you need. It's like the body unloads ballast for the spirit to rise. You don't need a squeegee and a bucket? No, we'd have noticed anything projectile. *(Laughs.)* I'm in such a good mood. Don't you feel better? I'll tell Dr Swan you'll call for him in one minute. Over the PA. Wash your hands.

GOVERNOR closes the door and WARDEN ALEX re-enters the execution room.

WARDEN SUNSHINE: What excuse did you give?

WARDEN ALEX: I literally have no idea.

WITNESS ROOM

SPIRITUAL ADVISOR: *(To AMY.)* Don't cry.

JOHN: My big brother's dead.

SPIRITUAL ADVISOR: Sorry, I meant her.

AMY: *(Referring to the JOURNALIST.)* I'm not talking in front of the scab.

JOURNALIST: I'm not a common-or-garden pap.

AMY: You crossed the picket-line.

JOURNALIST: I don't mean to offend you, but the strike is a sham. This morning, all the leftie papers published front-page articles about *refusing* to publish articles about today. Think about it.

AMY: It's out of respect.

JOURNALIST: How do you publicise a media boycott?

AMY has no answers for this.

Quite. If they had their way, he'd be in a Travelodge sipping Lapsang souchong, penning his autobiography.

SPIRITUAL ADVISOR: Don't you write for a left-wing paper?

JOURNALIST: I swing both ways. But seriously, *(To AMY.)* my readers are my moral barometer, and they give a damn about justice for your sister; they signed an e-petition. *(To AMY and JOHN.)* So you can all talk freely in front of me.

SPIRITUAL ADVISOR: *(To AMY.)* I wouldn't.

JOURNALIST: My middle name is Verity. *(To AMY.)* Verity means honesty. Truth is *literally* my middle name. *(Laughs.)* Ask my parents.

AMY: *(Quietly.)* Please shut up.

JOHN: Your paper wrote a spread about my mum and said she blackmailed money off her neighbours for her operation but she never because I paid for it.

JOURNALIST: That's different.

JOHN: How is it?

JOURNALIST: We stand by our sources.

PHYSICIAN: Did your mother *need* surgery?

JOHN: She had a tumour on her kidney.

PHYSICIAN: Had it metastasized?

JOHN: Had it what?

PHYSICIAN: Metastasis means the cancer spreads from one organ to another…

JOHN: It was a nasty tumour.

PHYSICIAN: Nasty maybe, but it must have been small. Financial assistance *once* the cancer has spread – that's the new value-for-money policy. 'Metastasized means subsidised.' It's a catchy rhyme, easy to remember.

JOURNALIST: Not so catchy.

JOHN: *(To PHYSICIAN.)* They turned her down on purpose because of the court case.

PHYSICIAN: Impossible.

AMY: I don't want to hear about his fucking mother.

JOURNALIST: *(To PHYSICIAN.)* At some point, Doctor, I'd love to bend your ear on the matter; maybe a quick interview?

PHYSICIAN: Really? Yes I'd love that…

SPIRITUAL ADVISOR: *(Interrupting.)* Let's have a moment of silence as we wait for the inmate's death to be pronounced.

JOHN: He has a name.

AMY: Why is this man in the same room as me?!!

JOURNALIST writes something down.

Enter GOVERNOR.

GOVERNOR: All done. The team are just cleaning up.

JOHN resumes sobbing.

(To PHYSICIAN.) They'll call you in one minute, Doctor. *(To everyone.)* Would anyone like a tea or coffee?

Lights down on the Witness Room.

Lights up on the Execution Room.

THE EXECUTION ROOM

WARDEN SUNSHINE: Obviously we have to ask the doctor.

WARDEN HEATHER: And tell him what?

WARDEN SUNSHINE: We can't just hide in here.

WARDEN HEATHER: You collect up your pot-plant and your mug if you want, but I need this job; I'm saving for a deposit on a flat.

WARDEN ALEX: A deposit? Oh sure. Are you cashing in your dental gold?

WARDEN HEATHER: Why are you being snobbish about my teeth?

WARDEN ALEX: *(Pointing at WARDEN SUNSHINE.)* Her *starter* salary's bigger than yours. They don't care about you.

WARDEN HEATHER: The governor said I had – QUOTE – 'a spark of talent.'

WARDEN ALEX: There's no smudges on my slate, that's all I'm saying.

WARDEN HEATHER: Do the checklist again. You might have missed something.

WARDEN ALEX: There's nothing to miss.

WARDEN SUNSHINE: Then why's he still breathing?

WARDEN ALEX: I used to write detailed reports for road traffic offences, so I think I can handle a thorough checklist.

WARDEN HEATHER: Just do it.

WARDEN ALEX: *(Reading from the clipboard.)* 'Syringe contents: Syringes 1 and 2 contain Sodium Pentothal. Syringes 3 and 6 contain Saline Solution. Syringes 4 and 5 contain Pancuronium Bromide. Syringes 7 and 8 contain Potassium Chloride.' Yeah? Yeah.

He turns over the page on his clipboard.

(Reading off the checklist, then answering the questions himself.) 'Do we have all designated members of our execution team?' Present. 'Has a designated team member ensured the chemicals have not reached or surpassed their expiration dates?' Tick. 'They have been stored securely at all times?' Yes, I just fetched them. 'A full simulation occurred one-week prior?' Last week, tick. 'A member has reviewed the inmate's medical file for any issues that could potentially interfere?' All clear.

He turns over the page on his clipboard.

And we did the drug test this morning.

WARDEN HEATHER: Do it again.

WARDEN ALEX: Come on…

WARDEN HEATHER: Cover our arses.

WARDEN SUNSHINE: *(To WARDEN HEATHER.)* Don't say it like that, say 'better to be sure.'

WARDEN HEATHER: Better to be sure we've covered our arses.

WARDEN ALEX: Step forward. Tongue out. *(Reading off the instructions.)* 'Oraline 98 Saliva Drug Test.' Sorry, it's this way up. *(Reading.)* 'The spoon is placed under the person's tongue and saliva is collected.'

As he is reading, WARDEN ALEX administers a presumption drug test (oral swab method) on WARDEN HEATHER and WARDEN SUNSHINE, and then on himself.

Now the breathalyser.

WARDEN HEATHER: Call it by its full name.

WARDEN ALEX: I am. It's called a breathalyser.

WARDEN HEATHER: No it's called the breath analyser. The breath analyser.

WARDEN ALEX: You're a lunatic.

WARDEN HEATHER: I don't do slang versions of important, official words.

WARDEN ALEX: Breathalyser is not slang for 'the breath analyser.'

WARDEN HEATHER: It's not my fault if you don't take your job seriously.

WARDEN ALEX administers a presumption alcohol test on WARDEN HEATHER and WARDEN SUNSHINE, then himself.

WARDEN ALEX: Waste of time. *(Back to reading the checklist.)* 'The telephone is fully functional? The PA system is fully functional? All syringes have been appropriately labelled and placed on stand A and stand B?' Yes, yes and yes. HAPPY?

WARDEN HEATHER: What's stand B for?

WARDEN ALEX: Backup.

WARDEN HEATHER: Let's stick him 7 and 8 again.

WARDEN ALEX: We can't give extra without permission.

WARDEN HEATHER: Stand B = Plan B.

WARDEN ALEX: That's not a phrase.

WARDEN SUNSHINE: I said to my dad, 'It's not creepy, it's an honour. Who wants to swivel keys when you could make history? *(Gesturing to WARDEN HEATHER.)* I'm working with the lass who executed the Westminster bombers.'

WARDEN HEATHER: *(For WARDEN ALEX's benefit.)* See? I've got credentials.

WARDEN SUNSHINE: No, I mean, this doesn't feel honourable. It feels creepy. I've stuck eight syringes into a man's arm and he's just sleeping.

WARDEN HEATHER picks up syringe 7 from stand B.

WARDEN ALEX: Put that back!

WARDEN HEATHER: Come on. He's a beached whale.

WARDEN HEATHER ignores him, and is just about to plunge the syringe when…

WARDEN ALEX presses the button to activate the PA system.

WARDEN ALEX: *(In a supermarket voice.)* Dr Swan to the execution room please. That's Dr Swan to the execution room.

WARDEN ALEX switches off the PA system. WARDEN HEATHER reluctantly returns the syringe.

WARDEN HEATHER: And we're sacked. Why did you use a supermarket voice? Can't harpoon him, can't throw him back in the sea. *(To WARDEN SUNSHINE.)* It's paint-by-numbers – *(Pointing at the syringes.)* they're *literally* numbered. It's like putting down a dog.

WARDEN ALEX: Is he a dog or a whale?

PHYSICIAN knocks on the door.

WARDEN ALEX opens it.

Apologies for the wait, we've had a technical hitch.

PHYSICIAN suddenly tenses up and refuses to walk in. He stands frozen in the doorway.

I'm the service manager for the execution team. *(Nodding towards WARDEN HEATHER.)* She prepared the drugs.

WARDEN HEATHER: Last week, in the PVC bags – before the rehearsal. They were checked. *(Accusatorily.)* Alex loaded the stands today. *He* filled the syringes.

WARDEN SUNSHINE: I did the injections in the right order.

WARDEN ALEX: *(To WARDEN SUNSHINE, witheringly.)* They're numbered one to eight; it's kind of Sesame Street.

WARDEN HEATHER picks up the saliva drug-testing devices from underneath the stands and holds them out to the PHYSICIAN.

WARDEN HEATHER: *(As if quoting from memory.)* We did the rehearsal one week prior and the checklist twice and the drugs test and the breath analyser and I have a first aid qualification level three.

PHYSICIAN: What kind of hitch?

WARDEN HEATHER: In terms of human beings…

WARDEN ALEX: *(Knowing the answer.)* On the heart monitor, the line is meant to go flat?

PHYSICIAN immediately presses the button to activate the PA system.

PHYSICIAN: *(Over the PA.)* Could the Governor please come to the execution chamber?

WARDEN HEATHER: Oh god! Please don't tell her!

PHYSICIAN runs back to stand in the doorway.

PHYSICIAN: I'm standing in the threshold, not inside the room. I'm not inside the room, I'm standing in the threshold.

WARDEN SUNSHINE: You will help us, won't you?

PHYSICIAN: I shouldn't even be standing next to this door.

WITNESS ROOM

GOVERNOR: *(Standing up to leave.)* There's my cue. Smoothly done.

AMY: Why are we still here?

GOVERNOR: He's not legally deceased until the doctor pronounces it.

GOVERNOR is leaving the room.

JOHN: Can I say goodbye?

GOVERNOR: You can visit his grave.

AMY: What's that?

GOVERNOR exits the Witness Room.

They're not burying him…?

SPIRITUAL ADVISOR: I believe it was a turn of phrase.

JOHN: In a nice plot, next to my dad.

JOURNALIST: *(Pen poised.)* Which cemetery was that again?

JOHN looks at the JOURNALIST with childlike suspicion.

JOHN: So you can tell everyone to swear on it with spray-paint and hit it with hammers?

AMY: *(To JOHN.)* Why don't you kill yourself?

SPIRITUAL ADVISOR: Amy…

AMY: What? You throw us in here together and expect us not to chat?

SPIRITUAL ADVISOR: I want you to know I have steered myself through a profound series of emotional storms and so I do empathise…

AMY: Go on then.

SPIRITUAL ADVISOR: Sorry?

AMY: Tell me how my pain feels.

SPIRITUAL ADVISOR: Right. Okay. I'll use a weather metaphor…

AMY: It feels like there's two tiny mouths behind my eye-sockets…

SPIRITUAL ADVISOR: *(To JOURNALIST.)* Get the wardens.

AMY: …but they haven't got vocal chords – they're just mouth-shapes without throats and their lips open with my eyelids, so I've got screams shining out my eyes. Is that what you were going to say? If you *empathise.* Fucking nob. *(To JOHN.)* Your family's scum, your town is scum, your street is scum, your voice is scum…

SPIRITUAL ADVISOR: Hey, hey, hey, hey! Justice has been carried.

AMY: Then why don't I feel better?

SPIRITUAL ADVISOR: Maybe, deep down, you're not actually a vengeful person.

AMY: *(Referring to JOHN.) Or* it's because he's here and he's alive and he should be dead too.

JOHN: Me? Why me? I'm good.

AMY: You're the same.

JOHN: *(Affronted.)* I am not.

SPIRITUAL ADVISOR unsuccessfully tries to position himself between AMY and JOHN.

SPIRITUAL ADVISOR: Hey now…

JOHN: I turned him in!

AMY: Three weeks after.

JOHN: I didn't know she was dying.

AMY: But you knew there was a girl in your house?

JOHN: I slept downstairs.

AMY: And you never heard a peep?

JOHN: He locked his room. Loud music.

SPIRITUAL ADVISOR: *(Overreacting slightly.)* Wardens! Now!

JOURNALIST strolls over to the glass and bangs with her fist, making ironic 'emergency' faces, pretending to slit her own neck.

AMY: I hate you so much.

AMY bangs her fists against JOHN's chest. He raises his arms to show he won't retaliate.

29

JOHN: She was dead when I found her; I pumped her chest.

AMY: Not enough! You didn't pump it enough...

AMY stops hitting JOHN and sinks to her knees.

JOHN *(Breaking down.)* I killed him.

AMY: Why don't I feel BETTER?

JOHN also sinks to the floor. AMY and JOHN grab onto each other – not fighting or hugging, just holding on.

WARDEN ALEX and WARDEN HEATHER run in. JOURNALIST is already sitting back down, writing in her notebook. Unnecessarily, WARDEN HEATHER grabs AMY and WARDEN ALEX grabs JOHN.

SPIRITUAL ADVISOR: *(To WARDENS.)* This whole ordeal should last nine minutes max, it's been twenty. They shouldn't be cooped in here. It's unhealthy.

JOURNALIST: *(Referring to SPIRITUAL ADVISOR.)* And he's no help.

SPIRITUAL ADVISOR: I am a big help.

WARDEN ALEX: *(To AMY and JOHN, putting on an official voice.)* Can I explain the...room dilemma? The only access to the main prison is through the car park and we can't guarantee your safety if we walk you through the protestors.

JOURNALIST: But it's non-violent. They're selling beads.

WARDEN HEATHER: Our cleaner had her jawbone shattered by a flying rock.

JOURNALIST writes something down.

WARDEN ALEX: *(To JOHN.)* You could wait in the disabled toilet? Or the cell?

Blackout on the Witness Room.

Lights up on the Execution Room.

EXECUTION ROOM

WARDEN SUNSHINE and the GOVERNOR are staring at RICHARD.

PHYSICIAN is hovering in the doorway.

GOVERNOR: We are *this* close to the go-ahead. 4.5 million. No more prefabricated huts. No more red plastic school chairs. A proper death row: modernised, equipped. Last year we had government officials swarming everywhere, this year – notice – they're letting us get on. As an institution. Normalising. 'The law's changed, let's continue' – that's the feeling we're trying to impart, okay? People don't often dish out compliments for executing, but if pushed they would praise *speed*. Send us your rubbish and we'll dispose of it. Efficiently. You won't smell a thing. I'm meant to be calling the Home Secretary right now. I'm meant to be proving my competence. *(Grabs hold of WARDEN SUNSHINE's arm.)* 4.5 million pounds. Are you listening?

WARDEN SUNSHINE: You're hurting me.

GOVERNOR: If we lose this funding…

PHYSICIAN: *(To WARDEN SUNSHINE.)* The funding's fine. What she means is – if she loses her promotion…

GOVERNOR: This isn't a closed, internal affair. Do you know what that journalist's name is? Grace Power. Never trust a reporter with a real name that sounds invented. Three questions: is he resistant?

PHYSICIAN: To deadly drugs?

GOVERNOR: Is he immortal? No. Then who's fault is this?

PHYSICIAN: *(Slightly smugly.)* As the inmate is still alive, I'd prefer not to engage in the off chance my words could help facilitate the means of unnatural death. I know you understand.

GOVERNOR goes up to RICHARD and slaps him in the face.

Ma'am, don't slap him.

GOVERNOR: You have no medical involvement. I'll do what I like.

GOVERNOR slaps him again.

Go home. Put your feet up.

GOVERNOR twists RICHARD's ear.

PHYSICIAN: One slight possibility is… *(Referring to WARDEN SUNSHINE.)* she may have missed his vein.

WARDEN SUNSHINE: What?

GOVERNOR: I knew it! *(To WARDEN SUNSHINE.)* You've soaked his soft tissue in poison.

PHYSICIAN: Speculation *not* diagnosis.

GOVERNOR: *(To WARDEN SUNSHINE, with total certainty.)* He's trapped in a miserable, fatal, spiralling coma.

PHYSICIAN: Maybe.

GOVERNOR: When I employ people like you, I don't expect them to perform the vital, fiddly tasks.

WARDEN SUNSHINE: People like me?

GOVERNOR: Equal opportunities people.

PHYSICIAN: Irrelevant.

GOVERNOR: Who designates the roles?

WARDEN SUNSHINE: Alex does, but ma'am you watched me through the window.

GOVERNOR: *(To PHYSICIAN.)* How is it irrelevant? She's obviously wobbled with the needle.

WARDEN SUNSHINE: Wobbled? I've wobbled?

GOVERNOR: Yes.

WARDEN SUNSHINE: I'm missing half an arm not half a leg. I don't *wobble* around.

GOVERNOR: Kindly alter your tone – my team consists of a half-armed lady, a black guy and an ex-prisoner who's clearly a dyke; if that's not inclusive I don't know what is...

WARDEN SUNSHINE: *(Overlapping.)* Wow.

GOVENOR: *But* – and I'm not being funny – if you can't clap you shouldn't really be administering injections.

WARDEN SUNSHINE: I can clap.

PHYSICIAN: *(To WARDEN SUNSHINE.)* I'm so sorry.

GOVERNOR: If you think that's clapping I'm not going to undeceive you, but let me remind you of our new law: 'The Irredeemable Crimes Act.' Parliament's first gutsy decision since politicians stopped smoking cigars over breakfast. First clause – obviously –

WARDEN SUNSHINE: Irredeemable.

GOVERNOR: The crime must be irredeemable. Thus, so far, we've had Guy Fawkes in a turban, two minions, and this chap. Clause two, however, pretty high up...

WARDEN SUNSHINE/PHYSICIAN: 'Death must be painless.'

GOVERNOR: Don't finish my sentences. *(To WARDEN SUNSHINE.)* Yes, we no longer tear folk asunder between two boats or tie them to mill-wheels. Britain has moved on.

PHYSICIAN: We're killing people.

GOVERNOR: Bad people.

WARDEN SUNSHINE: I didn't miss his vein.

PHYSICIAN: Last year was meant to be a one-off.

GOVERNOR: Define 'irredeemable.' Kill the bearded fanatics but save the evil white boy?

WARDEN SUNSHINE: I didn't miss his vein.

PHYSICIAN: *(To GOVERNOR.)* What's wrong with a simple overdose? Multiple syringes is just vengeful showmanship.

GOVERNOR: *(To WARDEN SUNSHINE.)* You'll probably get six years.

WARDEN SUNSHINE: In prison?

PHYSICIAN: Slow down…

GOVERNOR: *(Interrupting.)* What's your name?

WARDEN SUNSHINE: *(Almost in tears.)* Sunshine.

GOVERNOR: Birth name?

WARDEN SUNSHINE: Sunshine.

GOVERNOR: Oh dear. We gave you first-rate training, Sunshine.

WARDEN SUNSHINE: What about him? He's the doctor.

PHYSICIAN: I had nothing to do with it

WARDEN SUNSHINE: Exactly! If you weren't so bothered about your Hippocratic oath, they wouldn't have to train up amateur prison wardens to do *your* job and he wouldn't be dying in pain because of our mistakes.

GOVERNOR: Strangely articulate.

WARDEN SUNSHINE: *(Sobbing.)* I practiced on oranges. Hundreds of oranges.

GOVERNOR: *(Comfortingly.)* The jury will pity you.

PHYSICIAN: *(Disturbed by WARDEN SUNSHINE's distress.)* It's not her fault. I've changed my mind.

GOVERNOR: Doctor, have you made this dignified woman cry for no reason at all?

PHYSICIAN: Look, this is the execution: 1) Medical coma 2) paralysis 3) cardiac arrest. If he's still alive and not moving then – more likely, now I think of it – *(To WARDEN SUNSHINE.)* your fellow warden has misjudged the doses.

WARDEN SUNSHINE: *(To GOVERNOR.)* Yes! It's her fault! The gay girl with the gold tooth.

PHYSICIAN: *So* the muscle relaxant's suffocating him, the potassium chloride is burning his guts but he can't squirm because he's paralysed. He's in a cocoon of agony. I'm saying nothing more.

GOVERNOR: But he will die?

PHYSICIAN: Eventually.

GOVERNOR: Kill him for us.

PHYSICIAN: My ears needs cleaning. *(Declaring, as if to the world.)* I have not crossed the threshold of this chamber.

GOVERNOR: In primary school, were you the milk monitor?

PHYSICIAN: Why should I bend my principles?

WARDEN SUNSHINE: England chose the death penalty and you're part of this society.

GOVERNOR: She's brainy this one.

PHYSICIAN: England's wrong.

GOVERNOR: Piss off to Norway then.

WARDEN SUNSHINE: Yeah, why are you here?

PHYSICIAN: Damage control.

WARDEN SUNSHINE: What damage control?

GOVERNOR: Someone has to take responsibility.

WARDEN SUNSHINE: Blame the lesbian.

RICHARD: Responsibility.

Slight pause.

Hello. How are you today?

Pause. GOVERNOR doesn't take her eyes off PHYSICIAN.

WARDEN SUNSHINE: *(Switching on the PA.)* Could all team members please reconvene in the execution area?

Lights up on the Witness Room. Both rooms are now visible simultaneously.

(Witness Room.)

WARDEN ALEX: Sunshine, we're busy.

(Execution Room.)

RICHARD: Hello Sunshine.

(Witness Room.)

Silence.

AMY: Whose voice is that?

(Execution Room.)

GOVERNOR: *(With the lowest voice she can muster.)* Mine, the Duty Governor. Hello Amy. Hello Sunshine.

RICHARD: Hello Amy.

(Witness Room.)

AMY screams.

WARDEN HEATHER runs out.

JOHN: Richie?

WARDEN ALEX: *(To SPIRITUAL ADVISOR.)* You keep order.

JOHN: Richie!

SPIRITUAL ADVISOR: You would like me to *keep order*?

JOHN: Open the curtain! Richard!

SPIRITUAL ADVISOR: As in, physically restrain people?

WARDEN ALEX: Alright. Let's be peaceful.

WARDEN ALEX takes the executive decision to lock them into the Witness Room.

JOURNALIST: What the sodding fuck are you doing?

They go crazy. Obviously.

THE EXECUTION ROOM

GOVERNOR: Hello Richard.

RICHARD: Hello Richard.

GOVERNOR: The doctor's here to see you

PHYSICIAN is still standing in the doorway, refusing to enter.

PHYSICIAN: I'm just looking.

RICHARD: A cautious shopper!

WARDEN HEATHER: Is he brain-damaged?

PHYSICIAN: If there's moderate to severe cognitive impairment you'll have to call the judge and get a reprieve.

WARDEN ALEX: He wasn't impaired when we strapped him in.

RICHARD: I can't feel my hands.

WARDEN SUNSHINE: We secured him pretty tight.

PHYSICIAN: Unreasonable force.

WARDEN HEATHER: He was lying down to die. How's that unreasonable?

RICHARD: You have a beautiful red heart beating in a cage.

GOVERNOR: He's spouting gibberish. Use stand B; I'll get it signed off.

WARDEN ALEX: It's not on this clipboard.

GOVERNOR: Then please retrieve the correct clipboard.

Exit WARDEN ALEX, at a pace.

RICHARD: My head hurts.

PHYSICIAN: Often a side effect of lethal injection.

GOVERNOR: *(To PHYSICIAN.)* Now you're being sarky? You said *(Pointing at WARDEN HEATHER.)* she'd buried him alive in his own body.

WARDEN SUNSHINE: *(To WARDEN HEATHER.)* Don't worry, love.

WARDEN HEATHER: Me? What have I done?

PHYSICIAN: I could take him in for an MRI, but it's upwards from two grand and I'm guessing he doesn't have health insurance.

GOVERNOR: Why would he have health insurance?

RICHARD: Where's the nearest post office?

GOVERNOR: Hypothetically, if there were deterioration...

PHYSICIAN: Then ethically...

GOVERNOR: Tell me *legally.*

Enter WARDEN ALEX.

WARDEN ALEX: Ma'am, I've got the forms.

RICHARD: He's got the forms!

PHYSICIAN: You can't execute a person with brain-damage.

GOVERNOR: Abdul whatshisname was autistic.

PHYSICIAN: Abdul blew the legs off the Chancellor.

GOVERNOR: *He* killed a girl and kept her in a cupboard.

WARDEN ALEX: *(Unnecessarily.)* Wardrobe.

PHYSICIAN: It'll read differently.

GOVERNOR: Neither the prison nor the frigging P.M is going to pay for a scan to *save* Richard Sanger. Picture the headlines.

PHYSICIAN: Unless...

GOVERNOR: What?

PHYSICIAN: Nothing. I haven't got a Psychology degree.

WARDEN SUNSHINE: The counsellor has.

PHYSICIAN: *(To WARDEN ALEX.)* Get him.

GOVERNOR: Please don't give orders to my staff. I know you've had an energy drink and gelled your hair this morning but you sound ridiculous.

PHYSICIAN: I work in health care; I don't consume energy drinks.

GOVERNOR grabs the clipboard from WARDEN ALEX.

GOVERNOR: We've got two vending machines in that corridor. I've seen you. Biro!

WARDEN ALEX hands her a biro.

(To PHYSICIAN.) Diagnose or I'm signing.

PHYSICIAN: I'm not a psychiatrist.

GOVERNOR: Fine.

She starts to sign.

PHYSICIAN: Amnesia. Retrograde Amnesia. I think.

GOVERNOR: *(To WARDEN ALEX.)* Google it.

WITNESS ROOM

AMY, JOHN, SPIRITUAL ADVISOR and the JOURNALIST have all clearly shouted themselves into exhaustion. They are now slumped around the room, in various states of depression.

JOURNALIST: Don't breathe on me.

SPIRITUAL ADVISOR: I'm not breathing on you.

JOHN: *(Trying the door.)* I just need to do one thing.

JOURNALIST: You have this horrible, warm tangy breath.

SPIRITUAL ADVISOR: I'm sucking a sherbet lemon.

JOURNALIST: That's atrocious. That's an atrocious thing to be doing right now. Apologise to Amy.

AMY: I don't mind.

JOHN: He didn't look at me when he died.

AMY: He didn't die.

JOHN tries the door again.

JOHN: Yeah but when he did, he didn't look at me.

AMY: He's still alive.

SPIRITUAL ADVISOR: Can you sense it?

JOURNALIST: She heard his bloody voice you muppet! Why else have they locked the door? I hate that humming noise.

SPIRITUAL ADVISOR: There's no humming noise.

JOURNALIST: You can't hear it because you're slurping on pick and mix. It's not a cinema. Come on Amy, let's talk in the corner.

AMY: What for?

JOURNALIST: A little interview.

JOHN: *(Rattling the door handle.)* One thing.

SPIRITUAL ADVISOR: *(To JOURNALIST.)* Locked in a room with three fascinating stories; this must be wonderful for you.

JOURNALIST: Two stories. You're barely a topic.

SPIRITUAL ADVISOR: You know nothing about me.

JOURNALIST: If I documented your entire life for a year I could just about scrape together a decent joke. Now, Amy, let's talk about your beliefs…

SPIRITUAL ADVISOR: I am not a joke.

AMY: *(To JOURNALIST.)* You just called me 'a story.'

JOURNALIST: No, *he* called you a story. To me, you're a human being.

AMY: Oh well thank you very much.

JOURNALIST: You didn't let me finish – a human being of fine, unique character who has displayed tremendous…

AMY: *(Interrupting.)* Yeah.

SPIRITUAL ADVISOR: I said, I'm not a joke.

JOURNALIST: Amy, be honest, did you vote at the referendum?

AMY: No.

JOURNALIST: Is that because you were conflicted within your own conscience?

AMY: I was fourteen.

JOURNALIST: Yes of course.

SPIRITUAL ADVISOR: You're the joke. Do your research.

JOURNALIST: *(To SPIRITUAL ADVISOR.)* What's your area of expertise again, Mother Theresa?

SPIRITUAL ADVISOR: Well, that's an interesting question…

JOURNALIST: Here we go, buckle up…

AMY: Why are you being so rude?

JOURNALIST: I just don't like being trapped, okay? That's why I'm freelance, that's why I'm single, and that's why I carry a collapsible bike. I'm sorry, Amy, let's continue…

SPIRITUAL ADVISOR: In answer to your question…

JOHN bangs on the glass.

JOHN: HELP US!!!

SPIRITUAL ADVISOR: I do work from the teachings of Jesus and his disciples but I also follow Socrates and the spiritual savants, Buddha to the Eastern mystics right through to modern wisdom: Carl Jung, Ron Hubbard…

JOURNALIST: Chewing on the Eucharist in a Mosque facing Jerusalem.

SPIRITUAL ADVISOR: A bendy eyebrow doesn't make you wiser than me.

JOURNALIST: A bendy eyebrow?

SPIRITUAL ADVISOR: You're doing it now.

JOURNALIST: Seriously, don't piss me off.

SPIRITUAL ADVISOR: Oooh she's clicking her pen.

JOURNALIST: You're calling *me* cynical? Did you say a prayer with Richard Sanger? Did you sing Kumbaya before you sent him off to die?

SPIRITUAL ADVISOR: I provide the three S's: silence, solitude and spirituality. On the threshold of death, everyone deserves that.

JOURNALIST: Well-rehearsed. Smattering of applause.

AMY: Why does he deserve that? He doesn't deserve air.

SPIRITUAL ADVISOR: I see your point and I support everyone.

AMY: You can't support *everyone.*

SPIRITUAL ADVISOR: All of us cultivate angelic qualities; it's part of our human DNA, even if our souls become soaked in darkness.

JOURNALIST: DNA? Really? Do they test for fairy dust in semen analysis?

SPIRITUAL ADVISOR: No one values my contribution.

JOURNALIST: *(To AMY.)* He's baying for blood, peddling peace on the payroll of murderers.

SPIRITUAL ADVISOR: No one realises the toll it takes on my emotional health…

AMY: *(To JOURNALIST.)* Why did you call them 'murderers'?

SPIRITUAL ADVISOR: Ha! I told you she wrote for a left-wing paper.

AMY: I thought you were on my side?

JOURNALIST: This isn't about sides.

SPIRITUAL ADVISOR: My, my, she's a secret liberal.

AMY: *(To JOURNALIST.)* I thought your readers signed an 'e-petition'?

SPIRITUAL ADVISOR: Nice detail.

JOURNALIST: Yeah, well, if you want to bomb the BNP fancy dress party, sometimes you have to stick on a Hitler moustache.

SPIRITUAL ADVISOR: Are you calling me a Nazi?

AMY: So you lied?

SPIRITUAL ADVISOR: *(To JOURNALIST, referring to AMY.)* Are you calling *her* a Nazi?

AMY: When you said I could 'talk freely in front of you' you were just chatting bollocks?

JOURNALIST: Darling, no I wasn't – I care about your story.

AMY: So I *am* a story?

SPIRITUAL ADVISOR: *(To AMY.)* Yeah, *she's* the hypocrite.

JOURNALIST: *(To AMY.) He's* the one giving yoga mats to psychopaths.

SPIRITUAL ADVISOR: I thought I was 'baying for blood'? Make up your mind.

JOURNALIST: You make up your mind.

SPIRITUAL ADVISOR: I'm this institution's moral backbone.

JOURNALIST: You're the pole up the scarecrow's arse. Have some balls.

SPIRITUAL ADVISOR: Balls?

JOURNALIST: You said it yourself, no one values you.

Pause. JOHN tries the door again.

(To JOHN.) Did you go to school on the special bus? It hasn't unlocked itself.

AMY: Don't pick on him, you horrible bitch.

JOURNALIST: You told him to kill himself.

AMY: At least he's straightforward. You've just been sitting here, pretending to care about me, plotting your next headline.

JOHN: Can't they let us out just for one minute?

SPIRITUAL ADVISOR: *(Thinking to himself.)* Balls.

JOURNALIST: *(To SPIRITUAL ADVISOR.)* Stop breathing on my cheek!

AMY: *(To JOURNALIST.)* You disgust me.

JOURNALIST: Oh fuck off. You're not completely bashful when it comes to headlines yourself: 'My Half Life as a Twinless Twin,' – you've cashed a brown envelope or three; I *know* you have. Miss Amy Watkins. No one dares challenge the arrogance of the victims, but I see through your 'butter wouldn't…

SPIRITUAL ADVISOR: *(Interrupting.)* Okay! We all need to take a deep breath.

JOURNALIST: You don't. That's the only kind of breathing you fucking do. Close your mouth and hold your nose. Take some shallow gasps.

AMY: We needed the money from the tabloids to pay for the funeral.

JOURNALIST: And a new car.

AMY: My mum needed a car.

SPIRITUAL ADVISOR: *(With escalating conviction.)* You know what? This mud-slinging will have clean consequences, I'll use this opportunity honestly, I will fight back, I'll rise up against them, I'll swap sides and speak my mind: I have balls, I have two!

JOHN: I'm really really really really really really sorry.

JOHN wets himself – a dark stain spreading on his trousers. He simultaneously begins to shudder and cry.

SPIRITUAL ADVISOR: Urgh he's wetting himself.

JOURNALIST: *(Overlapping.)* Oh that's disgusting.

AMY: It's not his fault.

> *Blackout on the Witness Room.*
>
> *Lights up on the Execution Room.*

THE EXECUTION ROOM

WARDEN ALEX: *(Reading off his phone.)* Right, got it.
'Retrograde Amnesia…deficit in memory caused by brain-damage, disease, psychological…'

GOVERNOR: Nothing psychological.

WARDEN ALEX: … Can also be caused temporarily by sedatives and hypnotic drugs.

GOVERNOR: Yes! Temporary amnesia. The simplest answer is always the right one.

PHYSICIAN: That doesn't apply to medicine.

GOVERNOR: *(Interrupting.)* Either come in and join in, or stay outside and shut the fuck up.

WARDEN ALEX: 'Can be treated by exposing the patient to his own lost memories.'

GOVERNOR: Reminding him? *(Scoffs at PHYSICIAN.)* Is that it? *(To RICHARD.)* What's your name?

RICHARD: What's your name?

GOVERNOR: Are you playing games with me, Richard?

RICHARD: Ludo is a game.

WARDEN HEATHER: He remembers Ludo.

GOVERNOR: And how do you play Ludo, Richard?

> *Slight pause.*

RICHARD: With a mixture of sorrow and remorse.

GOVERNOR: He's mocking us.

WARDEN SUNSHINE: *Or* maybe he's collating fragmented feelings together; so the 'Ludo' is perhaps a childhood memory and the 'remorse' is connected to the crime but his brain has mangled them together?

PHYSICIAN: His brain has mangled them?

GOVERNOR: No that sounds right.

WARDEN HEATHER: That sounds right.

PHYSICIAN: Well who am I to question the top-down logic of such thorough deductive reasoning...

GOVERNOR: Do you feel remorseful, Richard?

RICHARD: A morsel?

GOVERNOR: Remorseful.

RICHARD: A morsel of bread...

WARDEN HEATHER: You know what she means, you lying bastard.

RICHARD: ...is a crumb.

WARDEN SUNSHINE: *(To RICHARD.)* Richard, do you remember when we chatted about the Storming of the Bastille and you growled and punched the door?

GOVERNOR: The whatting of the what?!

WARDEN HEATHER: This morning, she gave him a politics lesson.

WARDEN SUNSHINE: I was simply *alluding* to the historic significance of this event...

GOVERNOR: *(Interrupting.)* Are you writing a book?

WARDEN SUNSHINE: *(Quickly.)* What? No.

GOVERNOR: You're suspiciously well-spoken. If you're one of those corpse-sniffing criminology geeks, I'll skin you alive.

WARDEN SUNSHINE: Well I'm not.

GOVERNOR: I've never heard a warden say 'alluding' before.

RICHARD: I love the smell of rain.

GOVERNOR: Stand back. We're dealing with Retrograde Amnesia here, most likely caused by the barbiturates –

PHYSICIAN: You're making this up.

GOVERNOR: Let's assume the fatal component – 7 and 8 – didn't take, and the sodium bromide…

PHYSICIAN: Sodium Pentothal…

GOVERNOR: Caused a chemical reaction in the mind…

PHYSICIAN: Science fiction.

GOVERNOR: *(Ignoring PHYSICIAN.)* Thus once his cognitive functions have been fully restored by verbal memory exposure, the inmate should be fit to execute legally, and *(Looks at PHYSICIAN.)* ethically. Wardens, please explain Richard Sanger's crime so we can evoke his recollections.

Pause.

Go on.

WARDEN ALEX: Sorry, I…

GOVERNOR: Make him sane! Tell him why he deserves to die, so I can sign the dotted line without this wordy boffin jumping down my throat – sorry, oesophagus. *(To PHYSICIAN.)* How long is 'temporary'? Roughly? An hour?

PHYSICIAN: *(Suddenly simple.)* I'm not telling you anything.

GOVERNOR: Two hours? Three hours?

PHYSICIAN: Could be days or weeks…

GOVERNOR: You spiteful, petty, tiny man. This is sabotage. You know it's a 24hr warrant – I've got hours and minutes. *(To RICHARD.)* You are convicted of murder and rape.

RICHARD: What's a rape?

PHYSICIAN: Stop. There's a distinction between episodic and semantic…

GOVERNOR: *(Interrupting.)* Speak English.

PHYSICIAN: He might have forgotten what he did, but it's incredibly unlikely he'll have lost the actual meaning of words.

GOVERNOR: Amnesia's amnesia. *(To WARDEN ALEX.)* Tell him what rape means.

WARDEN ALEX looks at his phone.

You shouldn't need a search engine.

WARDEN ALEX: Rape is when you imagine doing something with a girl, and then instead of just imagining it, you actually do it.

Pause.

They look at him, appalled.

What?

GOVERNOR: Good try.

WARDEN SUNSHINE: Not quite the Oxford Dictionary definition.

RICHARD: Imagine doing what?

WARDEN HEATHER: It's violent sexual assault.

WARDEN ALEX: Not always violent.

WARDEN SUNSHINE: Excuse me?

WARDEN ALEX: Sometimes they're unconscious.

WARDEN SUNSHINE: I think you better shut up now Alex.

GOVERNOR: *(To RICHARD.)* Do you remember?

RICHARD: You're all such beautiful nurses in this hospital. Thank you for your kindness and support.

PHYSICIAN: This could be something more serious than amnesia.

GOVERNOR: Patronising, self-righteous…

GOVERNOR breathes deeply, and then turns to face PHYSICIAN.

I am the Governor of this prison. You are a medic.

PHYSICIAN: Physician.

GOVERNOR: There are many medics, many *(Like it's a dirty word.)* opinions. Next Sunday I'm having lunch with the Home Secretary. Why? The public have placed their trust in us to eliminate their vermin and today is just the edge of the verge of the beginning. I don't care how you voted at the referendum, the dirty protestors will *not* cycle home laughing, neither my parliamentary Sunday roast *nor* my prison's future will be compromised. This is a failed *medical* procedure. *You* are the important one.

PHYSICIAN: But I'm just a dispensable medic…?

GOVERNOR: *(Growling.)* Step into the room, Doctor.

PHYSICIAN: Make me.

GOVERNOR holds the PHYSICIAN's gaze for a moment.

GOVERNOR: *(To RICHARD.)* What's your name?

RICHARD: Ludo.

GOVERNOR: Right! Act it out. *(To WARDEN SUNSHINE.)* You be the girl.

WARDEN SUNSHINE: The girl?

GOVERNOR: Just do the highlights. *(To WARDEN ALEX.)* You be Richard.

WARDEN ALEX: What?

GOVERNOR: It's a spot of light role-play. You did drama at school, didn't you? Played a sheep in the nativity? You're Richard and she's the girl you raped, tortured and killed. Go.

PHYSICIAN: This is deeply immoral.

WARDEN SUNSHINE: I don't feel comfortable with this.

GOVERNOR: Are you with that guy? Are you a nay-sayer? Do you and him want to stand in the doorway like two disgruntled prostitutes?

WARDEN SUNSHINE: I beg your pardon?

WARDEN HEATHER: She was closer to my age.

GOVERNOR: *(To WARDEN HEATHER.)* Great. Thank you Warden – for being so mature.

WARDEN HEATHER beams.

You're Tara. Action!

WARDEN ALEX: Hang on, can we talk about this?

GOVERNOR: I swear – by all that is holy and innocent – if you can make him remember, I won't advise my friend the Home Secretary to prosecute all three of you for negligence.

WARDEN ALEX: Hello my name is Richard Sanger and I have invited Tara Watkins back to my house in London. We have only just met. It is the middle of the day.

WARDEN SUNSHINE: You're making it sound like a date. She wasn't 'invited.' She was dragged. Drag her by the hair.

WARDEN HEATHER: Not by the hair! Drag me by the collar.

WARDEN SUNSHINE: It's not as effective.

WARDEN ALEX: How should I act?

GOVERNOR: Improvise.

WARDEN ALEX: Improvise a rape?

GOVERNOR: Get her on the floor.

WARDEN HEATHER starts to lie down…

No, don't lie down voluntarily; it's not an antenatal class. Push her over Alex. Grapple her.

WARDEN ALEX grapples WARDEN HEATHER to the ground.

WARDEN HEATHER: Ouch, bloody hell…

GOVERNOR: Now lie on top of her.

WARDEN ALEX lies on top of WARDEN HEATHER.

No, you look like two exhausted walruses. Flip her over.

WARDEN ALEX: Flip her? Really?

WARDEN HEATHER: The floor's all dirty.

GOVERNOR: I just don't believe the violence. Where's the passion, Alex? Get in character.

WARDEN ALEX: The character of a rapist?

GOVERNOR: It's not difficult. She's a brainless piece of skin, she advances nothing except lip-gloss sales, she's barely worth her own spit and you want to rape her to death. Don't stare at me like that. I'm trying to inspire you.

WARDEN ALEX flips WARDEN HEATHER onto her front.

Good.

WARDEN ALEX rolls on top of WARDEN HEATHER, putting all his weight on her.

Now simulate copulation.

WARDEN ALEX: What?

WARDEN HEATHER: He's crushing me.

GOVERNOR: Thrust! Come on!

WARDEN HEATHER: Can't he rape me in missionary?

GOVERNOR: *(To WARDEN HEATHER)* No. *(To WARDEN ALEX.)* Hump her, pretend it's real.

WARDEN ALEX begins thumping his body against WARDEN HEATHER's back. She is clearly not enjoying herself.

Look at this, Richard. A young girl on the floor, kicking and struggling…

WARDEN HEATHER: I honestly can't breathe.

GOVERNOR: *(To RICHARD.)* The big strong man overpowering her…

WARDEN ALEX is getting a bit carried away.

WARDEN HEATHER: Time out.

GOVERNOR: *(To RICHARD.)* Cast your mind back.

PHYSICIAN: Oh my god.

GOVERNOR: *(Studying RICHARD's face)* I think he's remembering…

WARDEN HEATHER: Please stop.

GOVERNOR: Keep going.

WARDEN HEATHER: Time out, I said, time out!

GOVERNOR: Grab her by the neck.

WARDEN HEATHER: Fucking get off me!

WARDEN HEATHER throws WARDEN ALEX off her, and staggers to her feet, shaken and distressed.

GOVERNOR: Well you've ruined that re-enactment, haven't you? The fourteen year old didn't do that, did she? We wouldn't be here if the fourteen year old had done that. You stupid woman.

RICHARD: I want to go home.

GOVERNOR: Yes! Where's home? Where's home, Richard?

RICHARD: A house.

GOVERNOR: What house? Who's in the house?

RICHARD shrugs.

Your family?

WARDEN ALEX: His brother's in the Witness Room.

GOVERNOR: Can we bring him in?

WARDEN HEATHER: He's not quite right.

RICHARD: What's family?

RICHARD brushes against WARDEN SUNSHINE with the side of his head.

Hello Sunshine. Hello Amy.

WARDEN SUNSHINE: He's touching me.

GOVERNOR: Who's Amy?

WARDEN HEATHER: Twin sister.

GOVERNOR: His twin sister?

WARDEN HEATHER shakes her head. GOVERNOR has an idea.

Oh! I could kiss you. Identical twins! *(To PHYSICIAN.)* What's the medical word? Monozygotic? *(To WARDENS.)* Tara might be murdered but her face lives on; no more role-play, he just needs to *look* at her. Turn the gurney round to face the door. There's wheels on this thing, right?

PHYSICIAN: Halt!

PHYSICIAN walks into the room.

You've exploited my kind nature, twisted my advice, wrenched it out of context and now you've finally got what you desire, the medical professional has entered the execution room in the presence of a live condemned man and is now prepared – in the absence of any intelligently humane practitioners – to take control.

GOVERNOR switches on the PA system.

Lights up on the Witness Room

GOVERNOR: *(In a supermarket voice.)* Could all witnesses, emergency staff and personnel please be aware we are securing the building? Securing the building. Thank you.

GOVERNOR smiles at PHYSICIAN.

Over to you, Doctor. This entire incident is now your responsibility.

She slaps her hands together, ridding herself of all accountability.

All yours.

Blackout.

SETTING FOR ACT TWO

The stage is divided into three spaces: the Execution Room (stage right), the Governor's office (stage left) and a narrow corridor in the middle, with doors on either side.

THE EXECUTION ROOM:

A white leather gurney with straps.

A heart monitor (screen facing away from the audience).

Two wheeled 'stands' clearly labelled 'A' and 'B' (each designed to hold eight syringes in separate slots). Stand A is empty, and Stand B contains 8 syringes clearly labelled from 1-8.

A drip chamber.

At the back is a door marked 'Chemical Room.'

GOVERNOR'S OFFICE:

A huge wooden desk,

a corded telephone,

a tropical fish-tank

and a fancy coffee machine.

CORRIDOR

A red plastic chair (for waiting).

ACT TWO

SCENE ONE

CORRIDOR

AMY is sitting on a red plastic chair, waiting. She can't hear anything happening in either room.

EXECUTION ROOM

PHYSICIAN, WARDEN SUNSHINE and WARDEN ALEX are sitting around RICHARD (who is still strapped to the gurney). They have clearly been there for hours. There is a packet of biscuits on the go. WARDEN SUNSHINE is reading her Kindle.

PHYSICIAN: Kill.

RICHARD: Time.

PHYSICIAN: Death.

RICHARD: Sad.

PHYSICIAN: Scream.

RICHARD: Child.

PHYSICIAN: We're getting somewhere. Girl.

RICHARD: Friend.

PHYSICIAN: Once more. Girl.

RICHARD: Flowers.

PHYSICIAN: What makes you angry Richard?

WARDEN SUNSHINE: God, not again.

PHYSICIAN: Repeat the definition.

RICHARD: A strong feeling.

PHYSICIAN: A strong feeling of…

RICHARD closes his eyes.

Richard, wake up! Don't fall asleep, Richard.

RICHARD: Sorry Doctor.

PHYSICIAN: Displeasure! Anger means a strong feeling of displeasure.

WARDEN SUNSHINE: He's been awake nearly twenty hours.

WARDEN ALEX: So have we.

RICHARD: My belly hurts.

WARDEN ALEX: He needs a Twix.

PHYSICIAN: He doesn't need a Twix. Repetition should lead to elaboration. I feel angry when…

RICHARD: I feel angry when I feel a strong feeling of displeasure.

PHYSICIAN: NO!

PHYSICIAN breathes deeply.

RICHARD: Are you okay Doctor? Do you need another break?

GOVERNOR: *(Over the PA.)* Dr Swan to the Governor's Office.

PHYSICIAN opens a can of Red Bull and drinks with a hint of desperation.

WARDEN SUNSHINE: Steady on, that's your third.

Blackout on the Execution Room.

GOVERNOR'S OFFICE

GOVERNOR: *(Talking to herself, practising.)* Hello Home Secretary. I sincerely thank you for calling me back. *(Trying again.)* Hi Home Secretary, cheers for the call back, sorry for the late hour, there's been some last minute medical checks…

Enter PHYSICIAN.

PHYSICIAN: What kind of murderer talks about flowers and the smell of rain?

GOVERNOR: Don't bother knocking will you?

PHYSICIAN: We need an extension.

GOVERNOR: It's an execution, not a dissertation. 6am deadline.

PHYSICIAN: Believe me, he's a puppy.

GOVERNOR: *(Amused by her own pun.)* Deadline, funny.

GOVERNOR hands PHYSICIAN a piece of paper from her desk.

PHYSICIAN: What's this?

GOVERNOR: A short handwritten quiz.

PHYSICIAN: *(Reading.)* 'Do you remember using her corpse…' Oh my Christ.

GOVERNOR: All the puppy has to do is nod ten times, then we shred it.

PHYSICIAN: No. I don't know what those chemicals did to his brain, but that dark spirit has flown.

GOVERNOR: This is my latest, genius plan.

PHYSICIAN: This is human life, it's serious; you're being impossibly glib…

GOVERNOR hands him an A5 printed invitation.

And what's this?

GOVERNOR: Perspective. Compare the weights: *(Pointing at the quiz.)* that's ordinary print paper – 80 GSM, dispensable, but *this (Pointing at the invite.)* is over 250 GSM.

PHYSICIAN: What are you talking about?

GOVERNOR: Paper quality. Read it.

PHYSICIAN: *(Reading.)* The Home Secretary requests the pleasure of your company on 27th October…'

GOVERNOR: This Sunday.

PHYSICIAN: *(Reading.)* '…at the "Forces for Change" luncheon.'

GOVERNOR: They have to give these things names: 'Save the World Dinner,' 'Stop the Abuse Breakfast.' *(Quoting the invite.)* 'Dress code: smart.' Not formal, just smart – wear a jacket but bring a smile.

PHYSICIAN: *(Thrusting the invite back into her hands.)* I'm not intimidated by your posh invitation, and I'm not asking him these horrible questions.

Enter WARDEN HEATHER, carrying a pile of mobile phones.

WARDEN HEATHER: I've got loads of phones.

During the following exchange, WARDEN HEATHER hovers awkwardly near the doorway, waiting for the right moment to speak.

GOVERNOR: *(Taking it up a notch.)* This invite is a symbol. I am the future of the British justice system – 'Forces for Change' – I'm not being glib, I am caring for our country.

PHYSICIAN: For your career.

GOVERNOR: That's rich.

PHYSICIAN: Excuse me? I've compromised my entire professional reputation; I've broken my oath.

GOVERNOR: Exactly. If this leaks, you'll be a pariah, lower than a backstreet Botox merchant. Won't you? If this gets out…

PHYSICIAN: Are you threatening me?

GOVERNOR: You entered the execution room thinking you could do my job in a more humane way and now you're realising there is no other way but mine...

PHYSICIAN: There's mercy...

GOVERNOR: ...so you're back-peddling – for your *career* – with 'he's a puppy!' You promised to help me execute him and you can't shame me into letting you off just because you're failing. You're in this now. You're complicit.

PHYSICIAN: You *are* threatening me.

GOVERNOR: Come on, wouldn't it be convenient if he were dead? Cremate him tomorrow – all this flies up the chimney. Phew. Then I can get the funding for my state of the art execution wing, and you can go back to practising moral medicine.

They stare at each other.

WARDEN HEATHER: I've got loads of phones. I've got the cleaner's phones, I've got the security guy's phones, I've got *his* secret pager thingy...

PHYSICIAN: It's an electric thermometer. She knows it's an electric thermometer.

WARDEN HEATHER: *(To GOVERNOR.)* Will this bag do? It says 'Face of Fashion' on it.

GOVERNOR: Thank you darling, very thorough.

Exit WARDEN HEATHER.

GOVERNOR: *(To WARDEN HEATHER.)* Stay.

Enter WARDEN HEATHER. She hovers in the corner of the room.

PHYSICIAN: Why do you need a black bag?

GOVERNOR: Question number 10.

PHYSICIAN glances at the piece of paper.

PHYSICIAN: You know, I was almost persuaded... *This?* No way.

PHYSICIAN shoves the paper back into the GOVERNOR's hands.

I have my own firm and moral techniques.

GOVERNOR: Still clutching at those are we? Like a drowning monk in a mermaid brothel?

Slight pause.

I'll keep the lookalike waiting in a corridor. *(Smiles.)* On hand.

EXECUTION ROOM

WARDEN ALEX: Weird chapter names. *(Reading off the Kindle screen.)* The 'Tickler'?

WARDEN SUNSHINE: Huge metal claw that rips out hunks of flesh. It's a good read: 'The Theatre of Death: From Nailing to Necklacing.'

WARDEN ALEX: What's necklacing?

WARDEN SUNSHINE: They force a petrol-filled tyre round your chest then set it on fire. Very modern.

WARDEN ALEX: 'The Judas Chair'?

WARDEN SUNSHINE: A seat with a spike that goes right up your anus.

WARDEN ALEX: Sunshine, why do you have this on your Kindle?

RICHARD: That is not a chair.

WARDEN ALEX: Hey?

Enter PHYSICIAN.

PHYSICIAN: What are you doing?

WARDEN SUNSHINE: Chatting about history.

RICHARD: *(Upset.)* A metal claw doesn't 'tickle,' it makes you cry. It's mean to call things the opposite of what they are. A burning tyre is not a real necklace.

PHYSICIAN: *(To WARDENS.)* I leave the room for five minutes…

RICHARD: Are you a real doctor?

They stare at each other.

Enter SPIRITUAL ADVISOR.

PHYSICIAN: Not now.

SPIRITUAL ADVISOR: Why can't I come in?

PHYSICIAN: Get back behind the glass; stop escaping.

SPIRITUAL ADVISOR: *(Shaking his keys in the air.)* I'm autonomous, I work here…

PHYSICIAN: If there's a spiritual emergency, I'll send up a flare.

SPIRITUAL ADVISOR: In my humble opinion…

PHYSICIAN: What? Mister drama workshop? *(Imitating his voice.)* 'Richard, imagine you're a foetus. Is it warm and safe in there? How does the womb feel…?'

SPIRITUAL ADVISOR: *(Overlapping.)* I never said that.

PHYSICIAN: All you do is judge me and click your tongue. You're a joke. I know what I'm doing!

SPIRITUAL ADVISOR: I am not a joke! Why do people keep saying that? I just want to help…!

PHYSICIAN: I don't need any help!

PHYSICIAN pushes SPIRITUAL ADVISOR out and closes the door.

(To WARDEN ALEX.) Give him a Twix.

WARDEN ALEX feeds RICHARD a Twix.

RICHARD: *(Crying with gratitude.)* Thank you Doctor, thank you.

PHYSICIAN: Assault.

RICHARD: Pepper.

PHYSICIAN expresses his frustration (possibly kicks something).

CORRIDOR

SPIRITUAL ADVISOR: Hi.

AMY: Hi.

SPIRITUAL ADVISOR starts plucking up the courage to knock on the GOVERNOR's door.

GOVERNOR'S OFFICE

WARDEN HEATHER: That journalist said my frisking was 'borderline sexual.'

GOVERNOR: Everything's borderline here: we have latex gloves. Frisking is vanilla.

WARDEN HEATHER: She said she's claustrophobic and it stinks of piss.

GOVERNOR: Prison! Hello!

WARDEN HEATHER: But she's in the Witness Room.

GOVERNOR: Pass me that mug.

WARDEN HEATHER: Are you sure we can lock them in?

GOVERNOR takes out a large wooden box from beneath her desk. She removes the lid and pulls out a bottle of whisky.

GOVERNOR: This is my hurricane box, for special people.

GOVERNOR pours WARDEN HEATHER a large dose.

WARDEN HEATHER: Am I allowed?

GOVERNOR: Are you special?

WARDEN HEATHER downs the whisky.

Now listen, if I were a hack I'd tape phones to my legs and wear bell-bottoms so search her again, then *(Like this is crucial.)* make her a tea.

SPIRITUAL ADVISOR knocks on the door.

Hide the bottle.

WARDEN HEATHER hides the bottle behind the desk. GOVERNOR opens the door.

What?

SPIRITUAL ADVISOR: Let's examine the positives…

GOVERNOR: Is this a speech?

SPIRITUAL ADVISOR: No ma'am. Richard Sanger is a clean slate, literally, he's ours to sculpt, so let's start him again, from scratch, new name, new life. I'll give him classes in literacy, theology. Put me in charge of him.

GOVERNOR: This is a speech.

SPIRITUAL ADVISOR: Accidents can be transformative – think of Newton and his apple, Fleming and his fungus – so let's transform *this* accident into a turning point; something good, something…

GOVERNOR: *(Interrupting.)* What are you on about?

SPIRITUAL ADVISOR: A man without memory is a man reborn.

WARDEN HEATHER: He wants to foster a rapist.

SPIRITUAL ADVISOR: Mentor.

GOVERNOR: You're joking?

SPIRITUAL ADVISOR: *(Aggravated.)* I am not joking.

GOVERNOR: *(To WARDEN HEATHER.)* Make it a really lovely cup: separate milk, bourbon on the side.

Phone rings.

63

(Thinking it's the Home Secretary.) OH.MY.GOD.

WARDEN HEATHER: What about her notepad?

GOVERNOR switches off the PA system.

GOVERNOR: Is this button off?

WARDEN HEATHER: Yeah.

GOVERNOR picks up.

GOVERNOR: Governor speaking? *(Sighs with relief.)* Oh hello Roberta, I thought you were someone else.

GOVERNOR puts her hand over the receiver.

(To WARDEN HEATHER.) What were you saying?

WARDEN HEATHER: Miss Power's notebook…?

GOVERNOR: *(Into the phone.)* Hold on one sec. *(To WARDEN HEATHER.)* It's fine. There's a big difference between a soapy stain and a fresh pool of vomit.

WARDEN HEATHER: *(Alarmed.)* What?

GOVERNOR: So long as the news story is *resolved* when it hits the front page, the stink will be fleeting. Just keep her distracted. *(Into the phone.)* I'm afraid you'll have to make this quick. Who? Certainly not. It's our duty to call her, not visa versa. In due course. How's Timmy? *(Pause.)* Awwww. Got to go.

GOVERNOR puts the phone down.

Governor of Holloway. Push-over, advocates art by offenders. Contact request from Richard's mother; wants to know his last words, find out if he died peacefully…

WARDEN HEATHER: *(Trying to be matey.)* Ironic.

GOVERNOR: That's not what irony means.

SPIRITUAL ADVISOR: Can I just say…

GOVERNOR: *(Interrupting.)* You're very sweet.

SPIRITUAL ADVISOR: *(Trying not to explode.)* It's not normal to walk ten steps and lie down willingly to die, have you thought about that? I am not sweet, I am vital. I placate your beasts…

GOVERNOR: Stop it.

SPIRITUAL ADVISOR: I feed them enough meaning to keep their skin from shaking under your needles, but you know what? He's already *done* that walk…

GOVERNOR: You're spitting.

SPIRITUAL ADVISOR: He was saved. Something saved him! This is my chance to display my professional skills.

GOVERNOR chuckles.

GOVERNOR: Have a nap.

SPIRITUAL ADVISOR: DON'T YOU FUCKING LAUGH AT ME!

Pause.

GOVERNOR: Okay. After tonight you'll be moving on. Pastures new.

SPIRITUAL ADVISOR: I apologise…

GOVERNOR: Keys.

SPIRITUAL ADVISOR hands over his keys.

You'll never see me give cash to a tramp, or pose with a long-stemmed rose. I'm not a humanitarian with twinkling eyes. But I'm a manager. I manage people. I grease the wheels regardless of the vehicle, and long after your twinkling eyes have sunk, disappointed, down into the wrinkly folds of your beige face, I'll be stapling shit and I'll be sending emails.

GOVERNOR gives a book to WARDEN HEATHER.

(To WARDEN HEATHER.) Give that to the Journalist. *(To SPIRITUAL ADVISOR.)* You can find solutions together.

SPIRITUAL ADVISOR: What is it?

GOVERNOR: The Gigantic Suduko Puzzle Book.

Exit WARDEN HEATHER.

Exit SPIRITUAL ADVISOR, broken.

(Talking to herself.) Home Secretary, hiya, thanks for the lunch invite by the way, I'm thinking of getting it framed. Classy typeface. Who does your graphic design work?

CORRIDOR

AMY: Would you mind if I had a glass of water?

WARDEN HEATHER: Use the vending machine.

AMY: It just has… *(WARDEN HEATHER has already gone into the Execution Room.)* Red Bull.

GOVERNOR'S OFFICE

GOVERNOR: *(Talking to herself.)* Now *(Little laugh.)* sorry to talk shop but, you see, it's responsibility of our physician, no… of our in-house medical practitioner…

Phone rings.

OH.MY.GOD.

GOVERNOR picks up the phone.

Governor speaking? *(GOVERNOR puts her hand over the receiver and whispers 'Breathe, focus, control.' She answers and lets out an involuntary squeak.)* Hello! *(Clears her throat.)* Hello, Home Secretary. Sorry. Yes I know it's the middle of the… I *am* doing my job. It's our in-house *(Messes up her wording.)* physicianal… *(Receiving a bollocking.)* Yep. Yep. Yep. Why don't I call in the morn…are you sure? Your husband won't mind the phone? Separate rooms – very sensible, my parents actually…none of my business. Speak later then. How are the kids…?

The Home Secretary has hung up.

Shit.

(Talking to herself.) If I sounded flustered it's because we were bantering and…

She takes the whisky bottle from behind her desk. She pours a generous amount into her coffee, tastes it, makes a face, and then adds some more.

GOVERNOR'S OFFICE / EXECUTION ROOM

PHYSICIAN: *(Over the PA.)* Ma'am, we need to transfer him to a hospital.

GOVERNOR switches on the PA button.

GOVERNOR: *(Over the PA.)* You're very reliant on institutions, Doctor. Think of the stretcher-bearers on the Somme.

PHYSICIAN: *(Over the PA.)* Could you join me please?

GOVERNOR: *(Over the PA.)* Sorry what was that?

GOVERNOR dials the number of her own office into her mobile.

PHYSICIAN: *(Over the PA.)* Come here.

GOVERNOR: *(Over the PA.)* There?

PHYSICIAN: *(Over the PA.)* Yes please.

GOVERNOR: *(Over the PA.)* Oh no. It is not my place to enter into the execution room.

PHYSICIAN: *(Over the PA.)* You were in here this afternoon.

GOVERNOR: *(Over the PA.)* Was I?

She puts her mobile phone to her ear, the office phone rings.

One sec, my phone's ringing.

She picks up and pretends to have a conversation.

(On the phone, speaking to no one.) Governor speaking. Oh hello Home Secretary! Cheers for the call-back. *Of course* we won't exceed the warrant – any moment now we'll be clear for take-off, as it were. His name is Dr Swan, little chap, fresh out of school. Last minute medical checks or something. I *will* make sure he realizes the weight of his responsibility. How are the kiddies? The sack-race? How retro! I can't wait to chat development plans with you on Sunday. Okay then. Okay then. Bye now. Bye, ma'am, bye bye.

PHYSICIAN: *(Over the PA.)* Who was that?

GOVERNOR: *(Over the PA.)* Oh blast, did I forget to switch off the PA button? Damn, damn, damn. Please erase all pressure from your mind, don't worry about my crippling political burden.

GOVERNOR switches off the PA.

That's how it should have happened.

EXECUTION ROOM

PHYSICIAN: Smash.

RICHARD: Potato

PHYSICIAN: Dirty

RICHARD: Wellies

PHYSICIAN: Rubber.

RICHARD: Bouncy

PHYSICIAN: Breasts.

WARDEN ALEX laughs.

RICHARD: Chicken.

WARDEN ALEX: Bouncy breasts?!

PHYSICIAN: Coward.

RICHARD: Man.

PHYSICIAN: Cunt.

RICHARD: Can.

WARDEN SUNSHINE: What exactly are you trying to achieve?

WARDEN ALEX: He says 'bouncy' and the first word you think of is 'breasts'? Oh my gosh you need help.

PHYSICIAN: I was deliberately steering the game in that direction...

WARDEN SUNSHINE: If you don't mind me saying, Doctor, this could appear slightly juvenile.

PHYSICIAN: I've been trying for nine hours...

GOVERNOR uses her walkie-talkie this time.

PHYSICIAN jumps at the sound of GOVERNOR's voice coming out of his belt.

GOVERNOR: *(To PHYSICIAN, on her walkie-talkie.)* Just to say, that was my friend the Home Secretary on the phone. Over.

WARDEN SUNSHINE: There's a doppelganger in the building and you're choosing not to use her?

GOVERNOR: *(Over the PA.)* Warden 1 to the Governor's office.

PHYSICIAN: Don't call her a doppelganger. She's a fragile teenager.

WARDEN HEATHER runs into EXECUTION ROOM (from the WITNESS ROOM).

WARDEN HEATHER: I'm Warden 1, I'm Warden 1.

GOVERNOR: *(To PHYSICIAN, on her walkie-talkie.)* I explained the situation, and I gave her your name. Dr Brian Swan. Over.

WARDEN ALEX: I would have said 'castle.'

Slight pause.

Bouncy castle.

CORRIDOR

AMY: *(To WARDEN HEATHER.)* Could you tell me what's happening?

WARDEN HEATHER: *(Striding straight past.)* Sorry love, can't stop. I'm Warden 1. She just called Warden 1.

WARDEN HEATHER runs into the GOVERNOR's office.

GOVERNOR'S OFFICE

GOVERNOR: *(To WARDEN HEATHER.)* The doctor requested these questions. Say 'In case you want to prep.'

WARDEN HEATHER: 'In case you want to prep.'

GOVERNOR: Just like that *(Winks.)*

GOVERNOR pours another nip of whisky into a mug for WARDEN HEATHER.

Linger a moment. You have a *(As if she's searching for the perfect words.)* genuine glow about you. You remind me of myself; you're smart, you're savvy. Do you mind me saying that?

WARDEN HEATHER: Um, no.

GOVERNOR: Tell me, how long was your sentence?

WARDEN HEATHER opens her mouth to speak.

Don't be embarrassed. I've made mistakes, I just haven't been caught; we're the same you and me, we're equals, I feel you, I get you.

WARDEN HEATHER: Six years.

GOVERNOR: And how many years did you waver?

WARDEN HEATHER: Five.

GOVERNOR: What a motivating scheme. Has it been motivating?

WARDEN HEATHER: Yes ma'am.

GOVERNOR: Sit down for a second. Do you have a clean room on the grounds?

GOVERNOR pours her a top-up.

WARDEN HEATHER: Spotless. Are you not drinking?

GOVERNOR: My coffee's super-strong. You like it here?

WARDEN HEATHER: I love it.

GOVERNOR: You eat your tea in the canteen with your discount card?

WARDEN HEATHER: Breakfast, lunch and dinner.

GOVERNOR: And the other staff members tolerate you?

WARDEN HEATHER: What's that mean?

GOVERNOR: Some 'citizen' workers may feel their profession has been – I don't know – tarnished in some way; devalued.

WARDEN HEATHER: I'm a citizen.

GOVERNOR: Of course you are. What did you do?

WARDEN HEATHER: I sold heroin.

GOVERNOR: Chemicals. Now *that's* irony. Little lesson there. Off you pop.

WARDEN HEATHER starts to leave.

Oh and darling…

WARDEN HEATHER: Yeah?

GOVERNOR: I'm really proud of you.

Exit WARDEN HEATHER, speechless with joy.

(Over the PA.) I'm chatting with the twin now, Doctor. I await your final decision.

GOVERNOR takes out a travel-sized breath freshener from her handbag and sprays it into her mouth.

EXECUTION ROOM

WARDEN SUNSHINE: Use the clone in the corridor.

PHYSICIAN: We're not *using* anybody.

WARDEN SUNSHINE: Send her home then.

PHYSICIAN: I intend to.

Slight pause.

Why's the Governor giving my name to the Home Secretary?

PHYSICIAN opens another can of Red Bull.

Enter WARDEN HEATHER. She hands PHYSICIAN the piece of paper.

WARDEN HEATHER: In case you want to prep.

PHYSICIAN blinks at her.

GOVERNOR'S OFFICE

GOVERNOR: Please sit down in my chair. The adjoining neck-rest is particularly comforting. Coffee?

GOVERNOR goes over to her coffee machine and starts setting it up. She makes two expressos in special posh little cups.

AMY: We're not prisoners.

GOVERNOR: No one's here against their will. Amy, can I call you Amy? Nifty machine this.

AMY: You've locked the doors.

GOVERNOR: Two things are of paramount importance to me personally: your safety, and your security. Turkish delight?

AMY: Security and safety are the same thing, and I don't like coffee.

GOVERNOR: Oh. Two for me. I'll be zinging off the whitewash.

AMY: You can cut the White Witch bullshit with the sing-song voice. I'm eighteen now, I'm done with patronising therapy. You promised me you'd execute him at 5.30pm. You broke that promise. I knew there was a reason I didn't feel any better.

GOVERNOR: *(Changing tack.)* Okay, you got me. I was sweet-talking you; the coffee, the chair. It's desperate. It's dishonest.

AMY: I didn't say you were dishonest, it's just…

GOVERNOR: *(Interrupting.)* No I am, deeply. I never say this to anyone, but you remind me of myself. *(As if this is the deepest insight ever.)* Fractured yet strong – does that resonate with you?

AMY: Well, yeah…

GOVERNOR: I knew it would. Wounded yet resilient.

AMY: The government promised…

GOVERNOR: *(Interrupting.)* Amy, I remember when I first heard the news about your sister, that fateful morning: my radio alarm woke me with a stern voice, 'a body has been found.' I couldn't eat my muesli because I was so overwhelm…

Phone rings. GOVERNOR picks up.

Hello, Governor speaking? No please ma'am, call me at anytime. There will be no coverage. Why, has someone called? Of course they haven't: no leaks in this boat. I'll ring the moment…

Home Secretary has hung up.

(As if she's still on the line.) Looking forward to Sunday!

AMY: Did she hang up on you?

GOVERNOR: No. I've lost my trail of…

AMY: Bodies?

GOVERNOR: What?

AMY: 'A body has been found'?

GOVERNOR: My point is… *(Composes herself.)* death warrants expire, Amy. In normal countries, you get six weeks but our government is humane: so if the P.M dithers for a day, the inmate returns to his cell, drinks a Fanta, chats to his solicitor. All very fair on paper, but this is not a stay, Amy, this is a medical gaffe, and that man *cannot* regain his right to appeal. Drink the coffee.

AMY: I told you I don't like it. I have a question.

GOVERNOR: Where are your parents, Amy?

AMY: It's none of your business. Answer me this…

GOVERNOR: *(Interrupting.)* Confide in me. Tell me your troubles.

AMY: *(Getting flustered.)* No! Shut up! Richard Sanger won't remember anything when he's dead, so what does it matter?

GOVERNOR: You prepared that question, nice work – and I *completely* agree but it's the bleeding-hearts, Amy. They only care about protecting nutters, and that's why tonight is so important; we can't let them win.

AMY: What do you mean, win?

GOVERNOR: If this execution succeeds, I'll be made governor of the first modernised British death row. Doesn't that sound wonderful? No more meathead wardens playing at doctors, only the best staff, best facilities; separate witness galleries for relatives of the inmate and relatives of the victim…

AMY: Yes I want to officially complain about that…

GOVERNOR: *(Interrupting.)* Blame our weak-willed government, Amy, unable to finalise funding, unable to say 'yes, for sure, this bill will not be reversed.' That's why we're in this grotty prefab with crap amenities. We have to convince the Prime Minister he's made the right choice: the death penalty isn't out-dated or barbaric, it's easy – it's modern! It's here to stay. Do you understand how much hinges on this one, Amy? Do you understand the pickle I'm in?

AMY: You need Richard dead so you can get a better job and a better building.

GOVERNOR: Is that what you think I'm about?

AMY: I know when I'm being messed with. You want me as your poster girl.

GOVERNOR: I wish I were that mercenary. I wish I were that unfeeling and cold. *(Deep breath.)* Truth is, I'm too emotionally involved.

AMY: Bollocks.

GOVERNOR sniffles.

(Beginning to fall for it.) In what way?

GOVERNOR: Friends say 'it's just a job,' I say 'wrong, it's a crusade.' When you murder an innocent, a chunk of the world falls away and we *all* move closer to the edge. For years our cries were ignored but now true retribution is possible and I must lead this revolution – for you, Amy. For Tara.

AMY: You're very wordy.

GOVERNOR: We can't give those bleeding hearts any ammunition.

AMY: I didn't agree with capital punishment before.

GOVERNOR: Then wisdom stuck its claws in. I know, Amy, I know. Try the coffee.

AMY: Can I put sugar in it?

GOVERNOR: *(Smiling.)* Excellent idea, I have lumps.

GOVERNOR hands AMY a small pot of sugar lumps.

AMY: My mum has these.

GOVERNOR: *(Like this is an amazing coincidence.)* Does she really? I remember her face so clearly from the press conference, such brave cheekbones.

AMY: My dad did the press.

GOVERNOR: *(Interrupting.)* Of course. I remember his brave chin.

AMY: He left us.

GOVERNOR: Bastard. Have a special Italian biscuit.

GOVERNOR offers AMY a posh packet of biscuits.

AMY: Cheers.

GOVERNOR: Where's mum?

AMY: Squeamish of needles.

GOVERNOR nods sympathetically.

Yeah but she's a hypocrite because she killed my dog.

GOVERNOR: You mean 'put him down?'

AMY: Not really.

GOVERNOR waits for AMY to continue.

I got him for my fourteenth birthday. I couldn't be arsed to think of a name so I called him Doggie.

GOVERNOR: Lovely name.

AMY: He was my pet – not Tara's.

GOVERNOR: Okay.

AMY: My responsibility.

GOVERNOR: What the matter, Amy?

AMY: She got a bike instead.

GOVERNOR: Let it out.

AMY: I was conked out on the sofa after school so Tara said 'shall I take him to the park?' and I was like 'whatever.' I never saw her again. We found him chewing a tennis ball, on his own, dragging his lead. They found her in a bedroom two streets down, three weeks later.

GOVERNOR: Oh love.

AMY: The local paper cropped the wrong side on our yearbook photo and printed my face by mistake. I'm sorry. I didn't mean to tell this story.

GOVERNOR: Do you wish you'd walked the dog that day?

AMY: *(Eyes filling with tears.)* No.

AMY can't believe she's said this.

No.

GOVERNOR: It's alright.

AMY: It's not alright! She was me. She was the other one of me. And I'd have jumped under a train for her, no problem, bullet in the chest – but I couldn't die like that. Not like that. I don't want to die like that. I just couldn't…

AMY bursts into tears.

I'm sorry.

GOVERNOR: You don't have to want to be dead.

AMY: But I do. I do.

GOVERNOR takes her hand.

My mum murdered him.

GOVERNOR: What?

AMY: The day after they found Tara's body. Bam! Reversed over him twice. She said he could have barked and bitten – but he just let her go. We executed the stupid puppy.

Slight pause.

AMY looks at her.

Do you have your elbow on the intercom?

GOVERNOR: Don't be silly.

Enter PHYSICIAN.

PHYSICIAN: I'm so sorry about your sister. And your dog. I am truly sorry.

One of the mobile phones on the table suddenly starts ringing. The ring-tone is a loud, recognisable tune. GOVERNOR scrabbles to locate the right one.

(To GOVERNOR.) Can we speak in private?

GOVERNOR: *(To PHYSICIAN.)* No. *(Reading the phone screen.)* Number withheld.

GOVERNOR ends the call.

PHYSICIAN: We can't put these memories back in his head. They're desolate, they're depraved…

GOVERNOR: It's a nightmare he created.

PHYSICIAN: So what? It's still psychologically harmful.

GOVERNOR: Are you saying, we're fucking him up with his own thoughts?

PHYSICIAN: Whoever Richard *was*, the injections killed that man. He's lost.

GOVERNOR: Misplaced – and Amy is our shepherd.

AMY: Shepherd?

PHYSICIAN: Let's ask the brother instead.

GOVERNOR: You sexist piece of shit. Projecting your own fearful apathy upon this courageous young woman. She's been haunted sundown to sunset by night-sweats and 'what ifs,' but now she's here and she is ready.

AMY: Ready for what?

GOVERNOR: You've already surrendered, Doctor. Fingers in ears.

AMY: Sorry, what are you talking about?

GOVERNOR: *(To AMY.)* Tara was walking *your* dog, Amy. She was abducted. You were napping on the sofa. She was discovered; mutilated, propped up in a wardrobe like a roll of bloodied carpet.

PHYSICIAN puts his fingers in his ears.

You're still alive. Take some fucking responsibility.

AMY: Please don't say that…

GOVERNOR: You couldn't even be arsed to give him a proper Christian name. Doggie the dog? Shameful. Tara stood in for you – with her *life* – and now you can stand in for her, look out through your sister's eyes, resurrected, victorious, and you can say: 'Remember me? Fuck you! I'm going to watch you die.'

Without thinking, AMY immediately stands up and speaks.

AMY: I'll do it. *(Gulps, blinks.)* What do you want me to do?

GOVERNOR: *(Triumphant.)* Ask him.

PHYSICIAN removes his fingers from his ears and looks at them both.

Blackout.

EXECUTION ROOM / GOVERNOR'S OFFICE

While PHYSICIAN is reading the questions in the Execution Room, the GOVERNOR is preparing AMY in the office.

PHYSICIAN: *(To RICHARD.)* Do you remember that your name is Richard Sanger?

GOVERNOR: *(To AMY.)* You came here for redemption.

PHYSICIAN: *(To RICHARD.)* Do you remember watching violent pornography as a child?

GOVERNOR starts to put the black 'Face of Fashion' bag over AMY's head.

AMY: Why the bag?

GOVERNOR: *(To AMY.)* Trust me, please. It's all about the reveal.

AMY relents.

PHYSICIAN: *(To RICHARD.)* Do you remember your favourite knife?

GOVERNOR: *(To AMY.)* He's running from his own mind and we can't let him escape.

PHYSICIAN: *(To RICHARD.)* Do you remembering slicing through a young girl's fingers?

GOVERNOR: *(To AMY.)* We must turn him back into a murderer.

PHYSICIAN: *(To RICHARD.)* Do you remember anal rape?

GOVERNOR: *(To AMY.)* It sounds morally complicated but it's not.

PHYSICIAN: *(To RICHARD.)* Do you remember re-opening her wounds?

GOVERNOR: *(To AMY.)* You have Tara's face.

PHYSICIAN: *(To RICHARD.)* Do you remember your trainer pressing down on her neck?

GOVERNOR: *(To AMY.)* This is bigger than the law, bigger than my job…

PHYSICIAN: *(To RICHARD.)* Do you remember using her corpse for your sexual needs?

GOVERNOR: *(To AMY.)* This is about love, sisterly love…

PHYSICIAN: *(To RICHARD.)* Do you remember the judge declaring you 'inhuman'?

GOVERNOR: *(To AMY.)* Grown together in the same womb, bonded in birth. Warden, take it from here.

WARDEN HEATHER walks AMY through the corridor and into the Execution room.

PHYSICIAN: *(To RICHARD.)* Do you recognise this face?

PHYSICIAN whips the bag off AMY's head.

RICHARD and AMY stare at each other.

RICHARD: Kinda.

AMY collapses. She bangs her head against the syringe stand.

GOVERNOR: What did he say?

PHYSICIAN: Amy has collapsed.

GOVERNOR: Yeah but what did he say?

WARDEN SUNSHINE: *(To PHYSICIAN.)* She's clocked her head on the syringe stand.

PHYSICIAN: He said 'Kinda.'

GOVERNOR: Kill it, bag it and zip it.

PHYSICIAN: 'Kinda' isn't yes. I refuse…

GOVERNOR: *(Interrupting.)* I'm not chatting over a speaker.

PHYSICIAN storms through to the Governor's office.

WARDEN SUNSHINE: Doctor, there's a teensy bit of…
(PHYSICIAN has already gone.) blood.

GOVERNOR'S OFFICE

PHYSICIAN: 'Kinda' isn't enough.

Slight pause.

GOVERNOR: It's not enough?

PHYSICIAN: Of course it's not enough.

GOVERNOR: Well that's it then. We tried. I wanted to be Governor of Britain's first mega-jail, revered for my efficiency; but they can't choose me now. I'm tainted. I'm *(Like this is the worst human trait.)* inefficient.

PHYSICIAN: I don't care if you get sacked.

GOVERNOR: *(Picking up the office phone.)* I'll just tell them the truth.

PHYSICIAN: Who?

GOVERNOR: Everyone. The board. The BMA. The H.S. Game's up. I'll tell them about the amnesia and your heroic attempts to cure him, how you whipped the bag off Amy's head, and I'll say 'I'm sorry.'

GOVERNOR starts to dial.

PHYSICIAN: What does 'kinda' really mean do you think?

GOVERNOR: It means 'sort of.'

PHYSICIAN: 'Sort of' as is 'mostly.'

GOVERNOR: We can't deduce a confession with a thesaurus, but thanks for the effort.

PHYSICIAN: As in 'basically.'

GOVERNOR: *(Continuing to dial.)* I just need to make this call.

PHYSICIAN: As in 'practically' as in 'largely' as in 'almost entirely.'

GOVERNOR blinks at him, holding the phone.

If I 'kinda' remembered necrophilia, I'd be relatively concerned about my personal scruples.

GOVERNOR: So would I.

Slight pause.

PHYSICIAN: If I lose my medical license, I can't help sick children.

GOVERNOR: Shall I gently place the phone back on its cradle?

PHYSICIAN nods slightly.

GOVERNOR puts down the phone.

GOVERNOR: Picture this scene: Richard is dead. I open the doors to the masses, 'Everything's fine. We did what we promised,' and I don't mention your involvement; I don't mention you crossed the threshold.

PHYSCIAN: I'm just a white coat.

GOVERNOR: A shadow with a stethoscope. And this moral conundrum floats away.

PHYSICIAN: But the journalist will tell people.

GOVERNOR: She's locked in the Witness Room with the retard brother. She knows nothing.

PHYSICIAN: She knows we've been delayed for ten hours and – don't say retard – she heard his voice.

GOVERNOR: That warden messed up the doses; it's on her.

PHYSICIAN: We can't blame anyone without testing his blood.

GOVERNOR: Unwrap this for me would you?

GOVERNOR passes him a disposable breathalyser.

PHYSICIAN: I haven't been drinking.

EXECUTION ROOM

WARDEN HEATHER: Oh that's got a nasty corner.

WARDEN ALEX: There's those anti-collision rubber corner guards – they should use them. My mum has them on all the tables. Because that's a safety hazard.

WARDEN HEATHER: Any seepage from her ears?

WARDEN SUNSHINE: No.

WARDEN HEATHER: She's probably fine then.

WARDEN SUNSHINE: Thank you nurse.

WARDEN ALEX lies down on the floor.

WARDEN ALEX: Fuck a duck I'm tired. Wooah! It's just nice to have a moment, isn't it? Slice of peace.

WARDEN SUNSHINE: What if she dies?

WARDEN HEATHER: I'll tell you what's really nice.

WARDEN ALEX: Go on.

WARDEN HEATHER: Overtime.

WARDEN SUNSHINE: You're both fucking idiots.

WARDEN HEATHER: No, what I mean is, it's nice to feel needed, you know? Like you're really…the best. My brother said I should've done my stint and waited to come home, but it's all grey t-shirts and leaning by phones in prison; I was meant to work. I'm a *(Like it's a brilliant word.)* worker.

WARDEN SUNSHINE: You should get that tattooed on your face.

WARDEN HEATHER: I think I might ask for a raise.

GOVERNOR: *(Over the PA.)* Warden 1 to the Governor's Office.

WARDEN HEATHER: Ha ha! Suck on that, Sunshine. See? I'm Warden 1. I'm Warden 1.

Exit WARDEN HEATHER.

WARDEN ALEX: I'm just resting my eyes.

Long pause.

WARDEN SUNSHINE puts her ear to AMY's mouth.

She checks her pulse.

She appears satisfied by her findings.

GOVERNOR'S OFFICE

WARDEN HEATHER: But you gave me the drink…!

GOVERNOR: Am I wearing a party hat? What kind of Governor feeds whisky to her wardens on a work-day, during a crisis?

PHYSICIAN: *(Not looking WARDEN HEATHER in the eye.)* We believe you may have compromised the execution.

WARDEN HEATHER: How?

GOVERNOR: We'll figure out the details later. Remind me of your name.

WARDEN HEATHER: Are you joking with me?

Two of the mobile phones on the GOVERNOR's desk start ringing.

I've been here two years and you don't know my name?

Another phone starts ringing. Three phones are now ringing simultaneously, all with different, tuneful ring-tones.

PHYSICIAN: Why are all your phones ringing?

GOVERNOR: *(Reading off the screens as she rejects the calls.)* Caller Withheld. Caller Withheld. Caller Withheld.

WARDEN HEATHER: But I remind you of yourself…?

Another phone starts ringing.

GOVERNOR throws all of the mobile phones into her fish-tank. The water splashes over the sides.

PHYSICIAN: You'll damage your fish.

GOVERNOR: They'll get over it, they know me.

There is a loud banging on the window.

It's just the scabby protestors. *(To PHYSICIAN.)* Is she or is she not guilty?

PHYSICIAN: You have failed the breathalyser.

WARDEN HEATHER: *(To PHYSICIAN.)* Breath analyser. She said I was special. She poured it into a mug.

GOVERNOR: Oh you're definitely special. You're like a deer bleeding on the windshield of a van, wondering what's just happened.

WARDEN HEATHER: What *is* happening? Responsible for what?

GOVERNOR: Translation: I'm going to have to let you go.

WARDEN HEATHER: *(Panicked.)* No. You can't finish the job without me. I'm a *(As if remembering a quote.)* vital member of the execution team. I left my family, I left my mates; I left my whole world behind for this!

GOVERNOR: And what a world!

WARDEN HEATHER: THIS IS MY JOB!

GOVERNOR: Isn't sobriety a condition of your contract?

WARDEN HEATHER: Please don't talk about my contract.

GOVERNOR: *(To PHYSICIAN.)* She's violated the terms of her employment. We took her on trust, and she's sadly let us down.

WARDEN HEATHER: No, no, you can't send me back.

The office phone rings.

GOVERNOR: That'll be the H.S. Touching base.

GOVERNOR picks up.

Governor speaking? *(Pause.)* No comment.

GOVERNOR slams the phone down, visibly distressed.

WARDEN HEATHER: I'll do anything.

GOVERNOR: *(To PHYSICIAN)* A small flock of vultures may have gathered outside.

WARDEN HEATHER: A warden in prison is worse than a nonce…

GOVERNOR: *(Interrupting.)* She's exaggerating. She's drunk.

Another loud banging on the window.

GOVERNOR flings open the door and yells out into the corridor.

GRACE POWER YOU BACK-STABBING… *(In a blind fury, WARDEN HEATHER runs at the GOVERNOR and pushes her to the ground.)*

EXECUTION ROOM

WARDEN ALEX is napping on the floor next to unconscious AMY.

WARDEN SUNSHINE is reading her Kindle.

RICHARD: Sunshine?

WARDEN SUNSHINE: Yeah?

RICHARD: Will you read me that old poem again?

WARDEN SUNSHINE: You liked that did you?

RICHARD: I like the rhyming.

WARDEN SUNSHINE: Okay but don't fall asleep. *(Reading from her Kindle.)* 'My tale was heard, and yet it was not told,/ My fruit is fallen and yet my leaves are green:/ My youth is spent, and yet I am not old,/ I saw the world, and yet I was not seen./ My thread is cut, and yet it is not spun,/ And now I live, and now my life is… Oop. *(Reading.)* 'To continue reading, connect to a power source.'

Offstage, the sound of smashing glass. WARDEN SUNSHINE opens the drapes and looks through to the Witness Room (offstage).

Alex, wake up.

Lights up on Governor's office and Corridor.

GOVERNOR'S OFFICE

On the floor, GOVERNOR is straddling WARDEN HEATHER's chest and is about to punch her in the face when...

EXECUTION ROOM

JOURNALIST smashes through the glass.

She climbs through the window carrying a red plastic chair.

She has glass in her hair, and she's covered in specks of blood.

JOURNALIST: That glass should be shatter-proof.

Looking in amazement, she stalks through into the corridor.

CORRIDOR

The doors to the Execution Room and the Governor's office are both wide open.

On one side, JOURNALIST can see AMY's unconscious body.

On the other, she can see the GOVERNOR with her fist raised to punch her own employee.

As the JOURNALIST is speaking, JOHN (sprinkled with glass) jumps through into the Execution Room. He throws his arms around his brother. WARDEN ALEX and WARDEN SUNSHINE tackle him to the floor.

This isn't the article I came for. I was after normal feelings: clock ticking, tears. Gritty truth. Sunday supplement shit. This? This is amazing. I'm covered in glass. I warned that poncey half-wit to stop breathing on me. I just needed to know what was happening. Even as a pacifist I'm disgusted by everyone's incompetence. The hypocrisy in myself! Fascinating! As soon as I recover my sanity, I'll be a fucking powerhouse of opinion.

Enter SPIRITUAL ADVISOR.

SPIRITUAL ADVISOR: I wasn't breathing on her.

Blackout.

SCENE TWO

Lights up on the entire stage.

GOVERNOR'S OFFICE

5am.

The JOURNALIST is handcuffed to the GOVERNOR's chair, with the desk-lamp shining in her face.

In the middle of the room, JOHN is sitting on a red plastic chair. An empty chair is placed directly opposite.

PHYSICIAN is sitting on the floor in the corner, like a disgraced little boy, exhausted and broken. SPIRITUAL ADVISOR is sitting – in a similar state – in the opposite corner.

The phone is off the hook. Every so often, there is a loud banging on the window (the sound of press and photographers multiplying outside).

EXECUTION ROOM

AMY is still passed out on the floor.

WARDEN ALEX and WARDEN SUNSHINE wheel the gurney through the Corridor and into the Governor's office.

GOVERNOR'S OFFICE

WARDEN ALEX and WARDEN SUNSHINE un-strap RICHARD from the gurney, help him down and then handcuff him to the chair opposite JOHN. WARDEN ALEX takes a tape measure from his pocket and proceeds to measure JOHN and RICHARD's chairs exactly two metres apart.

The WARDENS wheel the gurney back into the Execution Room, before meeting with the GOVERNOR in the Corridor.

CORRIDOR

GOVERNOR: *(To WARDEN ALEX.)* Give her the checklist. You're swapping jobs.

WARDEN ALEX: Swapping?

WARDEN ALEX clings onto the clipboard.

WARDEN SUNSHINE: Oh god thank you ma'am, my heart couldn't take it twice.

GOVERNOR: I'm not doing you a favour. Alex is reliable. You've got the sly, squinty eyes of a novelist.

WARDEN ALEX: But it's not her designated role…

GOVERNOR: Give Sunshine the key to the chemical room.

WARDEN ALEX: I've never injected anyone before.

GOVERNOR grabs the keys off WARDEN ALEX's belt and hands them to WARDEN SUNSHINE.

GOVERNOR: I believe in you. Relinquish the clipboard.

Reluctantly, WARDEN ALEX hands over the clipboard.

WARDEN SUNSHINE opens the door marked 'Chemical Room' and exits through it.

Blackout on Execution Room.

GOVERNOR'S OFFICE

There is another bout of loud banging on the window.

GOVERNOR: *(To JOURNALIST.)* It's five in the morning. Do your monkeys never sleep?

JOURNALIST: *(This is not the first time she's said this.)* Why would I give away the scoop of the century?

GOVERNOR: Phil Hunter from *The Star.* 'Is it true you've lobotomised Richard Sanger?'

JOURNALIST: My Blackberry's in your fish-tank.

GOVERNOR: *(To JOURNALIST.)* You've concealed a secret device.

JOURNALIST: I'm a political columnist, I've talked about female circumcision on *Woman's Hour*, I don't have a phone up my arse.

They stare at each other.

GOVERNOR: *(To EVERYONE.)* John shall now proceed to provoke personal yet incriminating memories we couldn't possibly have forcibly 'implanted' and his brother's vocabulary shall extend beyond 'Kinda.' *(To RICHARD.)* Isn't that right, Richard?

Pause.

PHYSICIAN: Say 'yes ma'am'.

RICHARD: Yes ma'am.

GOVERNOR: Good boy.

GOVERNOR walks to the centre of her office.

JOURNALIST: Good boy?! What are you role-playing? Where's your mortar board and your sexy whip?

GOVERNOR: Are you finished?

JOURNALIST: You're darker than him.

GOVERNOR: I think the young man would like to speak.

She stands a step behind RICHARD and JOHN – like a referee for a staring competition.

Go.

JOURNALIST: Go?!

JOHN: Mum says you thought it was a film but then you woke up from the red cloud and it was too late.

JOURNALIST: A red cloud?

GOVERNOR: I buy that. Continue.

PHYSICIAN: He means 'red mist.' A feeling of extreme rage that temporary clouds one's judgement.

GOVERNOR: *(To PHYSICIAN.)* Your career is over, Brian. Stop interfering.

JOURNALIST: He kept her alive for three weeks.

GOVERNOR: Let the boy talk.

JOURNALIST: Long mist, that's all I'm saying.

JOHN: I'm sorry about your door, Rich, but you were out and I needed my jacket.

JOURNALIST: No one breaks a door down for a jacket…

GOVERNOR: Please.

JOURNALIST: *(Rattling her handcuffs.)* Please?!! You're saying please?!

JOHN: I couldn't smell blood!

JOURNALIST: Does he know why he's doing this?

GOVERNOR: I'm granting him the chance to converse with his Lazarus brother.

JOURNALIST: How compassionate.

GOVERNOR: *(To JOURNALIST.)* You're not leaving this room until I've proven his sanity.

JOURNALIST: What about yours? I'm handcuffed to a chair.

GOVERNOR: You vandalised my Witness Gallery like a crazed animal.

JOURNALIST: You locked me in a room for ten hours.

GOVERNOR: I gave you Sudoku.

The phone rings. GOVERNOR picks up a pair of scissors from her desk and snips the cord.

(To JOHN.) Carry on.

JOHN: My jacket was in the wardrobe so I opened it. I called an ambulance and said I'd found the girl off the television. They said is she breathing, I said her skin's grey, then mum came and she wouldn't look but she wanted me to cancel the call. They gave her two years just for panicking.

JOURNALIST: Sweetheart, no they didn't. *(To GOVERNOR.)* The day before, his mother paid a gypsy boy ten quid to heave up some paving slabs in the backyard. *(Proudly.)* I read the case-notes.

JOHN: She was gonna plant flowers.

JOURNALIST: Just three slabs. In an oblong shape.

JOHN: It wasn't a grave.

JOURNALIST: You're innocent, John. She's not.

JOHN: I didn't know the ambulance was connected to the police. I think it's because it's the same phone number.

GOVERNOR: *(To RICHARD.)* Talk to your baby brother.

JOHN: I love you.

GOVERNOR: Pretend we're not here.

JOHN: Rich, I couldn't lie to them.

RICHARD: *(Smiling.)* Look at your little face.

Pause.

Hiya.

JOHN: *(Overjoyed.)* Hiya.

RICHARD: I remember your chest rising and falling when you were baby. You made a toddler feel like a dad.

GOVERNOR: *(To JOURNALIST.)* Sorted.

JOURNALIST: Does he sound like a man who knows he's going to die?

JOHN: Can I have a hug?

RICHARD: I can't mate.

GOVERNOR: *(To JOURNALIST.)* He knows he's a prisoner.

RICHARD: *(To JOHN.)* It's just good to talk to you.

JOHN: *(To GOVERNOR.)* Can't you let him hug me?

GOVERNOR: No physical contact. We've measured you exactly two metres apart.

JOHN: Please.

RICHARD: Don't embarrass the poor lady. Do you remember in Anglesea when I wore those white shorts and I sat in a puddle of...what was it?

JOHN: Oh yeah. Crude oil.

RICHARD: Black, sticky stuff – that's it.

JOHN: It went right through your pants.

RICHARD: Mum made me sit in the back of the car, with my bits hanging out...

JOHN: You were cross.

RICHARD: It was funny.

JOHN: And we dunked you in the sea.

RICHARD: Blooming freezing.

JOHN: Then we played bat and ball.

JOHN starts to cry.

In the air, RICHARD mimes patting his brother on the knee.

RICHARD: There, there.

JOHN cries harder.

RICHARD starts to cry.

GOVERNOR: Right, well, he seems to have acknowledged his fate, let's...

SPIRITUAL ADVISOR: *(Interrupting.)* Pause to think, for once in your life.

GOVERNOR: But I've cured his amnesia…?

SPIRITUAL ADVISOR: By dawn break, he'll be nothing *but* a memory. Be kind.

PHYSICIAN: *(To SPIRITUAL ADVISOR.)* It's a bootless climb; forget it.

SPIRITUAL ADVISOR: *(To GOVERNOR.)* Be a human being.

PHYSICIAN: *(To SPIRITUAL ADVISOR.)* I tried that, doesn't work.

RICHARD: *(Through his tears.)* I'll see you in Heaven, mate.

JOURNALIST: Heaven?

SPIRITUAL ADVISOR: I told you he was spiritual.

Pause.

GOVERNOR: *(To JOHN, as if this is her independent idea.)* Although the world may disagree with my methods, I always respond to situations individually and instinctively; *(Looking at the JOURNALIST.)* jobsworths may use clichés like maverick or loose canon but I listen to myself, and my gut never lies. Tell you what. *(Dramatic, benevolent pause.)* You can hug for thirty seconds.

RICHARD and JOHN stand up and hug lovingly. They are both crying. Their foreheads are touching and their arms are wrapped around each other's necks (Although RICHARD's handcuffs makes his position look slightly more awkward.) It's a beautiful, moving sight.

Almost tearful, GOVERNOR looks at them both. As is her nature, she takes personal credit for this poignant moment.

PHYSICIAN: The healing properties of tenderness.

SPIRITUAL ADVISOR stands up.

SPIRITUAL ADVISOR: For myself and every member of the Worldwide Spiritual Advisory Council, this is a defining moment. A violent criminal branded 'irredeemable' by the British courts is hereby reformed through love. 'The Irredeemable Crimes Act' must be revoked! The premise is false! I was right. *(To JOURNALIST.)* Thank you Grace, for helping me rediscover my own truth.

JOURNALIST: No problem mate.

SPIRITUAL ADVISOR: We *can* divert our neural pathways to construct a whole new map.

JOURNALIST: *(To GOVERNOR, quietly.)* I wasn't trying to help him; I just thought he was a wanker.

SPIRITUAL ADVISOR: There may be no way back, but there's always a new way forward.

PHYSICIAN: Is that a quote?

SPIRITUAL ADVISOR: Nope.

PHYSICIAN looks at him, impressed.

PHYSICIAN: That's a serious point.

SPIRITUAL ADVISOR: I'm a serious person.

Enter WARDEN SUNSHINE.

WARDEN SUNSHINE: Ma'am.

GOVERNOR: Ten seconds.

WARDEN SUNSHINE: I don't know how to say this so I'm just going to say it. The syringes are full of water, and Alex is on the roof.

GOVERNOR blinks at her.

GOVERNOR: Alex is on the roof…

WARDEN SUNSHINE: And the syringes are full of water.

GOVERNOR: Water?

WARDEN SUNSHINE: Yes ma'am.

GOVERNOR: And chemicals?

WARDEN SUNSHINE: Just water. Evian water.

Slight pause.

GOVERNOR: *(Almost giggling.)* Evian water.

GOVERNOR laughs a little, in shock. She blinks. Then she realises.

WAIT!!!

Suddenly, everyone looks towards RICHARD and JOHN. RICHARD's handcuffs are around JOHN's neck, viciously strangling him. RICHARD's face has changed completely. His strength is clearly phenomenal, and his intent is obvious.

RICHARD: I really tried to reach out. In court they said I thrived on fear, how do they know that? Scared people are disgusting. They squeak like my mother. I like it when they give up, but you can't keep it in your wardrobe forever, it goes all raggedy. It didn't love me.

JOHN falls to the floor and RICHARD carries on strangling him, with his knee pressing down JOHN's chest.

Look at his little face. He's accepting the situation. I closed my soul and nothing happened, I thought – is this death? You lie there with your eyes shut, waiting to be cremated, and when your ash is scattered, you feel yourself flying through the air, mingling with the soil, – fully conscious – travelling through the body of a worm. But then I realised, someone's saved my life. Someone believes in Richard Sanger.

JOHN passes out.

It's alright, he's just unconscious. During my short prison stay, I've been branded 'uneducated,' the greatest insult of modern times, but I've simply been *reserved.* As a child, my mother said my tongue was 'touched by God.' Someone needs the gift of explanation in this dumb and gaping world. The penal system has never been about justice. Not really. Usually I'd begin with the Romans. The 18th century was bloodier than the 17th. A stolen pocket watch could deport a kid to New South Wales, a floating sardine-can full of paedos. Protect the pocket-watch owners! The industrial revolution: suddenly hard labour is pivotal. Break us down for parts. Now we've got the tabloid press. Indignation is big business. An eye for a sheep. A soul for a pocket watch. Anything but Norway! You research the Amygdala gland but psychopaths should rot in hell. Especially if they're Mancunian. Or missing an eye. We all need a punch-bag to stab. The poor deserve to be poor. The dying deserve to be dead. Is he calling himself a victim? You're distracting the public from their anger at the government. I'm irredeemable. Criminals are the perfect straw men: 'Look at this one. He's got a peg leg and a parrot.' It's like you've got this massive rat with a crown on his head, standing on a golden balcony and you're all gathered underneath, and this rat is declaring a crackdown on plague victims. You're watching rats on TV and you're reading rat books, and you're hosting dinner parties for herds of rats, and you're employed by rats in skirts. Diseased ones. *(Pointing at the GOVERNOR.)*

Pause.

JOHN groans.

He knew about the slut in the wardrobe by the way. He had a go on her. He just freaked out when she died – then he put all the blame on me.

RICHARD begins stamping on JOHN's neck. His violence is so terrifying, everyone steps back. Ridiculously, the GOVERNOR throws a stapler and a hole-punch at RICHARD's head. She misses. JOHN dies. GOVERNOR picks up the office phone then remembers she's snipped the cord. The mobile phones are in the fish-tank.

SPIRITUAL ADVISOR lifts up his shirt. A mobile phone is taped to his chest. He rips off the tape and calls 999.

(To SPIRITUAL ADVISOR, grinning.) You sneaky little fucker.

SPIRITUAL ADVISOR: *(Into the phone.)* Ambulance, police, ambulance, police…

RICHARD: *(Grins.)* He's definitely dead.

RICHARD grabs the GOVERNOR by the throat.

GOVERNOR: Richard, Sir, I do have influence in the judicial…
On Sunday I'm having lunch with the Home Secretary…

RICHARD: I love Sunday lunch. Beef and potatoes?

GOVERNOR nods.

No, do you think you'll have beef and potatoes? On
Sunday?

GOVERNOR: Oh, yes, beef and potatoes.

RICHARD: How comforting. Gravy and Yorkshire puddings?

GOVERNOR: A roast.

RICHARD: Home cooked?

GOVERNOR: She has an excellent chef.

RICHARD: With taxpayers' money?

GOVERNOR: Sorry, sorry, she'll cook it herself.

RICHARD: No you've put me off now…

GOVERNOR: Mr Sanger…

RICHARD tightens his grips around the GOVERNOR's throat.

Alright, alright. I'm an ambitious rat. Is that what you want
to hear? I step on heads to climb the ladder, but is that so
bad? You're a clever man. We've both got a philosophy
haven't we? What if I told you about my divorce, my
debts, my dying mother…?

RICHARD tightens his grip even more.

RICHARD: Irredeemable, baby.

GOVERNOR: There has to be another way.

RICHARD disagrees.

Blackout.

SCENE THREE

Ten minutes later.

The roof of the Execution Wing.

WARDEN ALEX is sitting on the edge, dangling his legs over the side.

WARDEN SUNSHINE walks up behind him, holding a small Evian bottle.

WARDEN SUNSHINE: You were careless with the chemicals.

WARDEN ALEX: I didn't think anyone would drink the dregs from old scabby bottles.

WARDEN SUNSHINE: I was parched; they were in the fridge.

WARDEN ALEX: Chemicals need to be refrigerated.

WARDEN SUNSHINE: In Evian bottles?

WARDEN ALEX snatches the bottle from her.

WARDEN ALEX: You weren't meant to go in there. She shouldn't have given you the key; the chemical room was my private domain.

WARDEN SUNSHINE: I rinsed my mouth out five times and my gums are still burning. Why didn't you just pour them down the sink?

WARDEN ALEX: What if they'd called in a specialist? What if I needed to change them back? I *was* worried she might ask you to execute him solo, but you've shown solidarity by coming up here; they're powerless without us and the death warrant expires at six. Three minutes! You're shaking. Are you cold? *(Pointing down into the street.)* Do you see the big banner down there? The knitted one? 'Inject Hope.' That's my girlfriend. And do you see the huddle nearest the gate? With the guitar? They're my old work mates from the CSOs. Community Support Officers. Don't get me wrong, I joined for all the right reasons, to *support* my community – but when they started asking us to ticket tramps for sitting on benches I thought, 'we're working for the crooks here.' This was all *my* plan. My vision.

The sounds of sirens in the distance, getting closer.

I was the mole in the hole, the ringleader. It's like a heist but instead of diamonds I'm stealing back our human rights. There's going to be a party down in the street tonight, rainbow streamers hanging from security cameras. *(Looking down into the street.)* Who's the ambulance for?

Loud sirens.

WARDEN SUNSHINE: Two ambulances.

WARDEN ALEX: Why do they need two ambulances? *(Looking down.)* And three police vans?

WARDEN SUNSHINE: Armoured cars.

WARDEN ALEX: Did the press kick off?

WARDEN SUNSHINE: John is dead. The Governor is dead.

WARDEN ALEX: Three ambulances.

WARDEN SUNSHINE: The journalist must be dead.

WARDEN ALEX: The police have guns. Why do the police have guns?

WARDEN SUNSHINE: Did you hear what I said?

More sirens.

WARDEN ALEX: Four ambulances.

WARDEN SUNSHINE: The doctor's dead.

In shock, WARDEN ALEX drops the Evian bottle.

I hope a thirsty hippy doesn't pick that up. *Five* ambulances.

WARDEN ALEX: It could be a safety measure…

WARDEN SUNSHINE: He ripped through Amy's shirt. She was laid out on the floor like a piece of meat. Alex, listen to me:

your moral crusade, swapping the poison for water and trying to save a man's life, I just want you to know…

Three loud gun shots.

I'm composing my criminology Ph.D on the benefits of capital punishment. *That* was the sound of the police *ethically* terminating the object of your noble campaign. Richard Sanger has now murdered five people and raped the victim's sister. Most likely, he died inside her. If we'd got him first, this tragic savagery could all have been prevented. Today has proved invaluable to my thesis.

WARDEN ALEX puts his head in his hands.

Finally! Sympathy for the prey not the predator.

WARDEN ALEX: If my sister were murdered, I'd want to kill the fucking bastard.

WARDEN SUNSHINE: There we go.

WARDEN ALEX: No! We need protecting from our hate. If the country absorbs it, we get a hate-filled country. Don't you get it? My mum never smacked. She sent us to our rooms. That's sane.

WARDEN SUNSHINE: My mum smacked me and she's sane.

WARDEN ALEX: She named you 'Sunshine.'

Big Ben strikes 6am.

Pause.

Blackout.

THE END